DEAD
LANDS

NÚRIA
BENDICHO
DEAD
LANDS

Translated from Catalan by
Maruxa Relaño and Martha Tennent

3TimesRebel

First published by 3TimesRebel Press in 2022, our first year of existence.

Title: *Dead Lands* by Núria Bendicho

Original title: *Terres Mortes* Copyright © Núria Bendicho, 2021
c/o Indent Literary Agency

Originally published by Editorial Anagrama S.A.

Translation from Catalan: Copyright © Maruxa Relaño and Martha Tennent, 2022

Design and layout: Enric Jardí

Illustrations: Anna Pont Armengol

Editing and proof reading: Greg Mulhern, Carme Bou, Bibiana Mas

Maria-Mercè Marçal's poem *Deriva*:
© heiresses of Maria-Mercè Marçal

Translation of Maria-Mercè Marçal's poem *Deriva*:
© Dr Sam Abrams

Author photograph: © Laura Rubio Troitiño

The translation of this book is supported by Institut Ramon Llull and Acción Cultural Española, AC/E

Printed and bound by TJ Books, Padstow, Cornwall, England
Paperback ISBN: 978-1-7398236-1-0
eBook ISBN: 978-1-7398236-5-8

www.3timesrebel.com

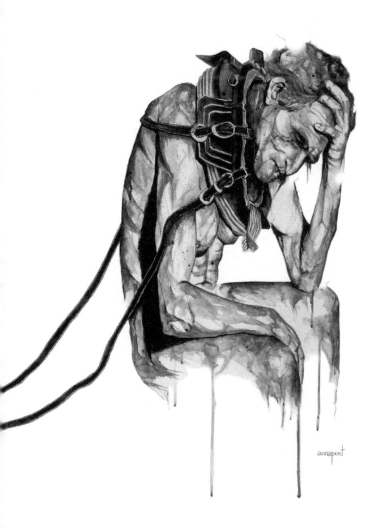

1
BOY

MOTHER'S EYES SEEMED MORE DEAD THAN JON'S. SHE PRESSED her son's knee with her left hand while cleaning her teeth with the other, using her fingernails to scrape them, right up to the gaps in her blackened gums. This had been going on for three hours. From time to time she swallowed the bloody saliva and resumed the task with greater zeal. My sister waltzed around, nursing the little girl while changing the water in the basin and placing damp cloths on the head of the dying man, who was in the throes of fever-induced delirium. I didn't know what to do with myself. Now and again I entered the room and watched for a while. Then I went outside and chewed tobacco with my father; sitting there in the shade, his silence made the wait all the more painful. And then like a traitor I would sneak away and traipse along the stream that watered the vegetable garden, and watch as my brothers, the men they were, worked the land even in such moments.

I remember it was a beautiful day, and only I had stopped to look up at the clouds. Long and thin, they faded away like the dark birds that swirled and fled, jackknifed and returned, back and forth without pause, never allowing my gaze to focus on them. The sun mottled my eyes with their black feathers. They screeched loudly and I followed them, screaming and jumping like a wild thing. That was my vigil. The longest wait of all, the same that sooner or later we would all have to face. I knew that while we kept this vigil, our own final moment of waiting was more present than ever. Death is death, the fear of it is the same for us all, and we know our turn will also come. His wait was long and painful. Every time I approached him he cursed, though at no one in particular, he had never been a belligerent man. My mother told me to pay him no mind, he was delirious; she said my brother spoke nonsense because he could no longer hear his own words.

The wind was the first to scream when a shotgun blast woke us the previous night. Then other strident, desperate cries led us past the hillock at the foot of the road to the stable. There lay Jon.

Father and Pere tried to lift him by the shoulders, but his legs wouldn't hold him. He couldn't stop screaming. I understood life was escaping through his mouth. They took him by the arms and tried to drag him. The screams continued. Pere stopped for a moment, stepped behind Jon's heaving body and grasped his feet to better carry him. Father resumed the march to the farmhouse. Maria followed them, eyeing the pools of blood that were left behind. Tomàs didn't help. Yearning to alert my mother I would run a few metres ahead, then would change my mind and retrace my steps, wishing to help Jon, who kept crying, Son of a bitch, son of a bitch!

We were back at the house fifteen minutes later. As soon as Mother saw him she ordered us to put him in bed. That's how he ended up here, in this horrid room that Mother spruced up for death. For three years no one knew where Jon was hiding. The day he turned up again, when Mother had long since mourned him as dead, she punished him by giving him the worst room in the house. Maybe that was why Mother didn't weep over him this time; she had already wept. It was the darkest room and also the smallest. The mattress was torn and the straw pricked the skin like needles. The cross that Mother had removed some time before hung above the headboard again. The room smelled of cold, of pain, of decay.

Now it was the child who whimpered in that room. Her mother couldn't hear her, she was too busy with her feverish older brother. I yanked her from her mother's breast. Maria always yelled at me when I dangled her by the legs like a rabbit. But this time she didn't say anything. I took her from the room. No one noticed us; not her mother, nor mine, not Jon, nor Father, who remained outside in silence; not even the dog, lying lifeless beneath the sun, on the scorched earth that wished to suffocate us, evaporate what was left of our blood. The day was violent, it was choking me. I hardly ever sweated, but the child always did. I couldn't stop worrying about her. Mother said she'd turned out sickly on account of the sin of her bad birth. Maria didn't even swathe her in rags, so I'd pee on the ground and make a mud wrap for her dark skin. So the hot sweat wouldn't escape through her pores. It was my duty to keep her from death. They say that whatever is created is meant to die, and every time the earth trembles a newborn dies. Even babies know this. I watched the earth and understood that wind, water and footsteps leave their mark, earth never remains the same. I was fifteen years old and no longer a baby, the little girl had no father and I was her uncle. I had to protect her from death.

That day for the first time she didn't sweat under the blistering sun, and once in my arms she stopped whimpering. I heard my father shout, ordering Maria to set the table. The shock had kept us from eating. My brothers also heard the call and dropped their tools.

The *escudella* had been in the pot for four days. The longer the stew settles the easier life in the fields becomes. But this remedy was powerless against the imminent loss of a child, and Mother preferred not to eat. She didn't even come in to get a whiff. The *escudella* was cold. Seated around the table, with each spoonful the family swallowed distrust, and with our glances we passed blame along, no one said a word. Only the child gave an occasional shriek. In this atmosphere of suspicion I realised the son of a bitch had to be one of us. I lost my appetite. Or it lost me.

Mother came into the kitchen. She said it was all over. A stream of tears cleansed her grimy cheeks. I had never seen Mother cry. She wasn't like Maria. Tears are made of water, and water is where wayward women die; in the sodden depths a woman sees herself, lost within herself, her sorrows drown in whirlpools of water, all the dreams that will never be. Maria was a wayward woman. And I spied on her when she entered the pond naked. She dropped her towel on the marshy earth and after wetting the bar of soap, she caressed her body with it and sank into the water. I knew she was afraid of wanting to stay there forever, she always hesitated before taking the first step in. She had a beautiful body, much more beautiful than Mother's. Her face too. I knew this because I'd once seen Father blowing the dust off an old photograph, his eyes filled with grief. Then he hid the picture under his tobacco tin. It was my mother at Maria's age, less pretty but with the same veil of sadness, standing next to my father and a man I believed was my grandfather.

But Mother didn't weep the way Maria did. My sister would be crying when she came out of the pond, she would have to rinse her face three more times. The same when she dressed the little girl. At night we all had to suffer through, but no one said anything to her. She never looked you in the eye. And her sorrow was contagious. I knew she wasn't like that when she was small, she told me that we'd spent hours playing together, she said this with such nostalgia that it pained me. She told me I should be filled with laughter, and not have children yet, lest one day I search for childhood memories, and not finding any, despair at their loss, when really I had been the one to ruin them. But it was hard for me to laugh, and when she was melancholy I had to look after the child. I think you should live as if you're already dead. If you're dead Maria can't drag you into the abyss. But I was alive and couldn't escape Maria's sorrow, and it was my brother who was dead.

In the kitchen everyone suspected everyone else, except Father, who seemed more in love with Mother than ever, and with bulging eyes begged her compassion. Father had always been a good man. Now he was like an orphaned child. I would have hugged him. Not Mother, she had no intention of embracing him, nor did she seem to notice he was observing her. She only stared at Tomàs, her favourite, seeking solace for a mother who would walk in death for the rest of her life.

Maria asked to be excused, ignoring the stew, which she hadn't tasted. I decided to follow her. I found her looking at Jon. Mother hadn't even closed his eyes. The child shrieked from afar, loud and persistent. Maria watched the dead man with her head bowed. The light seemed to reflect only the tainted paleness of death. Darkness oozed from Jon's mouth, as if with his last breath he'd expelled the sadness of all those years. The black viscosity stained the bedsheets. His fist was clenched, fingernails dug into his skin.

Without a word, without so much as touching him, Maria left and went outside. I was like a dog, always following everyone. The fields were parched. The air was hot. The sun yellowed the leaves, the dry leaves and the ones that still clung to life. She left her shoes under the doorframe and walked on barefoot. The earth burned. Her feet burned. Her hair was aflame and soared into the air, wanting to escape her screams, but it couldn't, you can't escape your rightful place. I, too, wanted to scream but couldn't, my whole body was suffering, my teeth bit my lower lip. Father came out. Like me he said nothing, like me he did nothing. Maria leapt about, her feet jumping faster, and the child continued to wail. Pere emerged and gathered her in his arms. He carried Maria as if she were the child. I ran to her and grabbed her feet. I squeezed them with ferocious intent, to stop the weeping. I wanted to slap her because this time I couldn't stand her tears. She wasn't weeping over Jon's death; she was weeping for herself. Now she was alone. Truly alone. Her tears were interlaced with screams. And the child continued to wail, but only I could hear her.

Maria gradually settled down and Pere released her; he pulled her closer by the hair and held her against his chest. He told her not to worry, we don't ever completely die. Nothing dies completely. Pere was sweating a lot, I would've been disgusted. And Maria was yelling at us, saying we didn't understand. We knew who had killed him and we didn't understand. It was the same person who long ago had killed us all. Every one of us. But I didn't know who had killed him or who had killed me or that I was dead. Mother came out and slapped her. Everything was reduced to silence, air, earth, fields.

Father sat on the front steps with the child on his knees. Two globs of mucus, painfully excreted, landed on the little girl's head. Father had always smoked a lot. He said we didn't have a coffin, someone should go down to the village and find one. It was a long journey. We lived far from everything. I'd only been to the village twice, and I'd seen things there I would've liked to see again. But now I didn't want to go. I didn't want to abandon Jon, and I was afraid I'd come back and someone else would be dead, or the murderer would kill me on the road and the cicadas would sing with pride and eat me and pester me like on the mornings when they kept me awake. Mother said animals eat bodies once they're dead. She'd seen it with her own mother. Maybe that's why Pere said we never completely die. Because flies, worms and cicadas would soon have some of Jon. And from now on Jon would sing with the cicadas every day to remind me he was dead, and it would be harder for me to forget him.

The only one who hadn't budged from the table was Tomàs. All he did was work. He almost never spoke. At night he smoked with Father under the stars, but they didn't speak. Neither of them talked much. They looked alike. First-born sons look like their fathers. Jon was the one who always talked to me, maybe he was the only one who had something to say, having been away for three years and seen more of the world than I had the two times I'd been to the village. Father had never been beyond the village or the county line. Nor had Tomàs, and I was sure he never would because he was over thirty now and already old. And he had no wife or children. Nor words, enthusiasm, or kindness. I always thought he hated me because he never played with me, and yet sometimes I caught him gently stroking the baby. And when I looked him in the eyes he always held my gaze until he scared me off. He'd throw the pack of cigarettes on the ground if I asked him for one, as if he didn't want to touch me. As if he was ashamed of me. As if he found me disgusting. It was a surprise when he volunteered to go to the village to look for the pine box. Pere said no, he couldn't do it alone. Father insisted on accompanying Tomàs, but Maria said he was too old. Father set the little girl on the ground and said he needed to do it himself. No one had anything to add to that, and the two of them set off together.

From the farmhouse we could see lots of mountains. They rose mightily, but the heat made them tremble in our eyes. The rocks looked sickly and were covered with dead shrubs. Hard rocks with black freckles. The sun killed everything. And out of the blackness sprouted dry threads of puny life. Lavender and thyme. Maria hung sprigs of lavender all over the house and sometimes boiled them in a pot, the way she said witches did to calm their nerves. The day Jon returned she caught him sniffing the bouquet by the front door. Tomàs must have seen him coming because he was busy with the tomato plants along the road, but he didn't say anything to him, and I ran out to meet him. I was standing on a rock inspecting some ants and I tripped and fell into a bunch of prickly leaves. Jon removed the thorns before greeting me, and told me not to worry, blood was a lot like life, it flowed out slowly and a time came when you no longer cared. That's what it was to grow up. I plucked some bluish lavender grains and started munching on them.

He was dark when he came back. His skin very brown, his hair very black, his nails very dirty. He was the only one in the family with green eyes. Green eyes that are ever vigilant, he said. He had some bread and chorizo in his bag. I remember the wind was blowing hard, and his hair wanted him to stop talking to me, it attacked his eyes and he paused and closed them, and ran his hands across his face. We had gone beyond Roca Negra because he wanted to see me before he saw the others. Hidden away there, the two of us ate the bread and chorizo, and the ants smelled my reddened fingers without daring to bite me. After each anecdote, Jon smiled as if it grieved him to be back and gently touched my cheek.

He didn't tell me why he had left or why he'd returned. The days passed very slowly for me. I've learnt a great deal, he said, damn if I haven't learnt some things. He'd seen a blonde woman. He'd met her in a boarding house where he had worked for a while. The men gave her money and she spread her legs for them. I didn't understand why men would pay her to spread her legs. He said that one day I would, and I should try it then because it was even better than gazing at the stars or getting out of bed and stretching your arms to loosen up. That when a woman spread her legs there was no sky, no men, no time, none of the reasons that force you to flee. He told me again that he understood Tomàs better now, though he couldn't forgive him, nor did he know why he himself was here, why he'd returned, maybe it was because I was still at home. I was glad he was back, I just wanted to play with him. I wanted to show him the little fishes I'd made with the mud from the stream, how they dissolved when you tossed them into the water. The figurines disintegrated and the earth returned to the source.

Intrigued by his stories, I too wanted a woman to spread her legs for me. It wasn't until three days later that I asked Mother to do it and she yelled at me, What have they told you, and my glass of milk crashed to the floor and she stormed out and no one cleaned up the mess for two days. The milk gave off an awful stink and dead ants were stuck to it.

It was Maria who cleaned it up. I know because she called me in a loud voice and when I got there she scolded me. If I did it again she'd beat me, she'd beat me or make me pay for the milk. And I said all right, it would never happen again, if I'd said anything else she'd have started on me right then. She was always yelling like that, if you didn't know her you'd think she was born evil. But evil people don't cry. Only suffering people cry. I didn't know what the matter was with her, but sure enough, when I looked at her I saw pain. And it was hard for me to ignore, because we were blood, and we ate under the same roof.

I was the first of the siblings to learn she was pregnant. Like a stable boy who followed her wherever she went, I'd gone with her to wash clothes. I watched her from a distance, seated on a tree stump that had been clumsily cut by unknown hands; these lands were ours alone and the axe wound was too inept to have been done by any of us. My chin hairs were coming in and I was trying to yank one out, furiously clenching my jaws. As I held up my head I couldn't help but see her. She had started to make strange movements, dancing around like a madwoman, and she gave animal-like whimpers. A bee was pestering her. She lifted the paddle she was using to soften the clothes and began swatting at it. I yelled at her to stop, it's when you hit them that they sting. But she didn't listen. She charged at it, swatting as if possessed, and her bare feet started bleeding from the sharp stones by the stream. Those stones had rolled down from the mountains, Pere said, they were the kind that broke off with the cold.

When she stopped screaming, I went over and gathered the knickers she'd been washing and in her fit of hysterics had dropped in the mud. They're soiled again, I said. As well they should be, she replied. There was a silence I didn't understand, and then she said they should be bloodied. When there's no blood there's a baby. Who told you that? Mother did. And who's the father? It won't have one, and it's your mother's fault. She stressed it was my mother, as if she wasn't hers as well, as if repudiating the womb that had carried her. The only thing I thought to ask was if she wanted the baby. I want it to die and for me to die as well. She said nothing more. She grabbed the wash paddle with the muddied panties and crouched over to finish the chore.

Jon had just left at the time. He didn't say goodbye to anyone. Pere said the word in the village was he was holed up in the mountains, preparing for a war we all knew was coming. Do you believe that? I asked. Not really. Not at all, in fact. Jon departed and summer arrived. The cicadas sang again. As always, the fields of dead grass were washed with amber. The hours passed slowly and the dog was dirtier than ever. My eyes were trained on the dog when Mother announced she had to go to the village. Can I come with you? Yes, but hurry up, it's a long walk and I want to be back before dark.

That was the first time I went to the village. Mother didn't speak on the way there or offer any explanation. I didn't understand why we were going if we weren't taking anything, and I couldn't think of a reason that might explain our visit. No one ever went to the village without a reason. Especially not a woman like my mother, who didn't much like people, particularly if they wanted to share their troubles, and villages are always filled with people. She had enough looking after herself, herself and Father, though really she couldn't stand him. He was a man who spoke too slowly, and her mind was too fast.

There was very little shade on the way down. I remember worrying I'd be sunburned like the day before, when my skin had turned beet red, so I pulled down my sleeves and held my scarf over my face with my teeth. If I turned my head even a little the skin under my ears started to feel tight. Mother walked awkwardly, as if she might twist her ankle at any moment. When we stopped to rest I found a lizard's tail. I closed one eye and held up the tail, trying to block out the sun without much success. The tail was stiff and rough. I showed it to my mother. She smiled at me, the way she did when she wasn't paying attention but something inside her still wanted to listen. My tongue had been itching for a while. I put the tail in my mouth like a piece of sweets, and scratched my tongue on the scaly skin. It helped.

The village was the same brown colour as my house. The holes in the stone walls were inhabited by long-legged spiders and dust. We entered on Main Street. This is Carrer Ample, she said. It's called that because it's wide. There's a Carrer Ample in every village. We walked the length of it, almost to the end. Children younger than me were playing in the street; when they saw me they stopped and glanced at each other, as if wondering whether to laugh at me or throw stones. It was the first time anything like that had happened to me and I would have liked to move along faster, but Mother had me when she was older and walked like an old woman. So I went past with my head down, eyes almost closed, like I was counting steps and couldn't hear their laughter, the dead thud of the ball that halted the game so they could look me up and down.

The women of the village had decorated their windows, the fountain, and the ground around the square with plants and flowers. Most of the flowers were white or red or a pale shade of yellow. The earthenware pots were brown and varnished, the larger ones on the ground, the smaller ones in the windows. I liked the contrast of the green stems and thick leaves against the earthy ground. The women were gathered in the square, seated on poorly woven straw chairs and wearing house smocks. The older ones had hunched backs. The younger ones, knees held apart, ate cherries to cool off and spat out the stones between their legs. They took turns speaking, with long pauses, and kept their brows furrowed, their faces canted, that was all the blood-orange afternoon sun would allow. They laughed without smiling, almost like they were shouting and breathing in at the same time. An open door offered the only view of shade. Every now and then a bee buzzed in my ear, or I caught a glimpse of a dragonfly sniffing the water in the fountain, which was filled with stones, twigs, floating leaves. Almost there. Where are we going? The church.

Mother had never been to the church before. She said it was for morons who don't know what's what. Did you come to pray for Jon? I don't know how to pray and I don't want to pray. God doesn't need this, and whatever I do or don't do, He's not going to lose any sleep over it. So, why did you come? You just sit by the door and wait for me. And I sat on the steps because I always did what she said, because I'd never learnt to do the things others did so I stopped trying, because I was the only one of the children who'd never heard from her that there was always a task waiting to be done.

Three months had passed since we'd last seen a black raincloud, and the heat at that hour was unbearable, even for the toughest of beasts. But the heat didn't enter the church. Only the white sunlight did, an intense brightness that fell on the dirty plaster walls of the one building in the village with a carved door. It was a thick door though not that heavy, it wasn't hard to push open; it squeaked but the sound was for my ears alone, no one else was inside the church. The windows were small and rather high up, but there was more light there than at home. Everything was nice and tidy: two lines of small pews stretched from my feet to the altar, beyond which stood two statuettes, one on either side. They cast shadows like I'd never seen before: fainter, not as dark as those in the country, as if more refined, and the shadows danced in the white light that flooded everything, pursued everything but me, for I advanced slowly through the stillness, heading nowhere in particular, breaking up the light without being inside it. I had just noticed a woman carved in wood, weathered, faded, gazing down at her baby, when I heard something that might have been a sound but wasn't. A soundless cry, born of someone in great distress. Someone who was near me, whose breathing I could feel, a silent breathing that nevertheless I perceived. I followed it, trying not to drag my feet, not to be seen, for I feared my mother might discover me and punish me with her indifference.

And I wasn't wrong. The man looked at my mother with atrocious fear, the kind of fear I felt when I walked alone in the mountains and the wind roared and it was like a black monster pursuing me, making everything quake and quiver, spitting out moans and scratching at the leaves, and all I could think to do was to search everywhere for that monster, as if my fear would diminish if I looked it in the eye, or finding the monster would somehow protect me. Mother was the monster that day, and the man was unwilling to look away, to blink even for a second, lest he lose sight of her. But then I coughed, and instinctively the man looked at me, and when he saw me his eyes widened, and inside him there was no longer fear but anger, a deep rage directed at me, soundless but keenly felt, because I made him avert his eyes from the monster and the monster seized the opportunity to devour him. Or maybe it wasn't fear, it wasn't anger. It was shame, as he would admit to me years later, when I'd discovered he was a priest, the day he ran off to vomit after Tomàs began to saw Jon's dead body, and I followed him. It's the one thing a man does not grow accustomed to and never will, he said. It's what he will try to wipe from his face to no avail, because when least expected, the agonising thought returns that one day he will be found out. I didn't know then what the man was talking about, or the meaning of shame, the only thing that had me worried was that he might vomit during the funeral. I didn't want to miss Jon's burial on account of having to clean up the mess.

But the man wasn't completely off the mark. When he arrived that morning, atop the wagon that carried Jon's box, along with Tomàs, Father and a boy I'd never seen before, he still had that ossified expression of shame on his face. It was clear he hadn't come to terms with things. Maria had spent the morning anxiously going about the house chores, I figured she'd wanted to get a head start to keep her mind off that agonising time, with Jon's body still lying in plain sight. But when she finished she took a chair and sat in the sun in front of the house, her gaze fixed on the point where the road vanished. Every time I spoke to her she replied curtly, as if I was bothering her, and to distract myself I started playing with the child. Maria never stopped fidgeting, and when she glimpsed that black dot slowly approaching from afar she bolted from her chair. As it drew nearer, the spot turned grey and revealed the tired mules pulling a tired wagon with all the men. Maria took the child from me and ran inside to hide her. She returned alone and started dusting off her dress and tidying her hair, with her hands and sleeves she wiped the grease from her face. The wagon with the men grew larger, disappeared down a hill and reappeared larger still when it crested another hillock, until at a certain point it ceased to be a stage set and became something concrete, embodied, and not just with one body, but several. They had almost reached the house when Pere emerged. Maria remained motionless, like a stone in the road, and he grabbed one of the mules by the neck and stopped the wagon before it could run her over. Tomàs handed him the pine box and Pere lifted it without any help, he set it on the ground and started laughing. Tomàs told him to shut up, it was the only box they could find and it would serve the purpose. But Pere continued to laugh. And Tomàs, from atop the wagon, kicked him in the shoulder and told him to help Father down, he was exhausted. While I watched my brothers, the priest had managed to get his feet on the ground and now he was standing beside me, though I didn't notice him until he asked about Jon. Mother hasn't even closed his eyes, I said. He still had that look of shame, the only thing for which men cannot forgive themselves, and suddenly the unfamiliar boy interrupted the conversation, he jumped out of the wagon and asked where my brother was, smiling sweetly in order to get past the priest. He'd never seen a dead man. I didn't want to go back into the room, so I just pointed and started walking and they followed me. I left them there, the three of them alone, not quite understanding what they wanted with Jon or why they'd come up the mountain to bury him. I started looking around the house for the child, but I couldn't find her. I stumbled on Maria, who said Mother was looking after her, trying to make her sleep and not be a nuisance. I didn't want to see my mother, so I asked Maria if she needed help with anything, and she said we should build a fire. With everything that had happened that morning, she'd forgotten the firewood, but a few twigs would do, and would I go with her. We headed to the woods, her hair still down, lustrous in the wind. I didn't ask why she had dressed up to receive Jon's box. It was a strange day, but we took our usual path: a small path that started near the house, and grew steep after a few metres; you had to zigzag down if you didn't want to fall, until you reached a clearing where the sun dried out the dead branches discarded by the oak trees and the ground grew harder and harder. I'd been wearing my house smock with the big pockets for days, all I had to do was follow my sister and she'd fill them with whatever kindling we could find. My pockets weren't quite full when she said, Wait, maybe we should offer them something to eat. And me: I have a bellyache, you do it. And she: I'm asking you as a favour, you do it. And me: we have enough to start the fire now, I'll come back for more firewood later. She stroked my face in appreciation, and we climbed the slope again, her free hand grasping mine to keep me from falling. When we got home, Father and Tomàs had started digging Jon's hole by the vegetable patch and Pere was tending the lettuce. We went straight to the kitchen and set the wood on the stone ledge beside the fireplace, she arranged the branches so the

air would flow between them and I blew on them, and together the two of us stoked the flames. We finished the job,
and she said that when the stew boiled I was to call the priest
and the boy—his name was Esteve—and offer them a bowl,
and if there wasn't anything left in the pot when they finished, I should fry up some meat and put it aside for the
family, because it was going to be a long day. That's what I
did. As I waited for the stew to boil, I scraped the dry food
from the plates with my fingernails, and once the dishes were
clean I put them on the table, not perfectly set but at least
the right number. One plate for each. And then the stew
boiled and everything was ready, I'd even wiped the crumbs
off the table with the back of my hand. My first impulse was
to call out, but I changed my mind because I didn't want to
wake the child, so I went to look for them in the room where
Jon was laid out. The priest gave a start when I addressed
him, as if his thoughts had taken him far away; he apologised
and said he wasn't hungry, he'd just had a butter sandwich.
Esteve was the hungry one, he pushed past me like it was his
house, almost knocked me over following the smell of food.
I can take what I want, right? No, I said. I grabbed the dish
from him and served it myself. Here, it's too hot and I can't
hold it with one hand, eat up. I looked into the pot and almost
nothing was left, just a bit of broth, a few chickpeas and some
chicken scraps. I cut some pork into strips and put it in with
more water, and reheated it so the fresh meat would cook
and there'd be food for the others. Can I have a second
helping? There isn't much left. As if he didn't believe me,
Esteve rose from the bench and came over to peer into the
pot. He took a wooden spoon from his pocket and began to

scrape the bottom to remove the crust of dry broth, and after being at it for a while he put the spoon in his mouth and began to suck on it like it was sweets. It's s-s-s-so good, want to try? Disgusting. And when he'd licked the spoon clean, he put it back in the pot and he pulled out a ham bone, plucked it out with one hand and put it straight in his mouth. But the whole bone wouldn't fit, and he probed every bit of it with his tongue, licking off the salt, and held it with his hands so his teeth wouldn't lose their grip on it. This lasted and lasted, until he'd had his mouth open so long that he started to retch, he had to spit out the bone and kneel down so the blood would flow to his head again.

The dog dashed for the ham bone Esteve had dropped, and by then I'd had enough. I told him to tidy up when he was done, I couldn't pay him any more attention because I'd promised my sister I'd fetch more firewood. He stopped looking at the dog and came over, put his clammy hands on the back of my neck and said he'd come with me, he'd always liked the woods. I told myself that maybe in the open air I wouldn't notice his stench so much, maybe then I could tolerate him.

Just as we were leaving the farmhouse the child's crying resumed. I didn't want to check on her because I knew she was with Mother, and I'd been avoiding Mother since the previous night. I didn't want her to burn me with the candle again. But the little girl kept crying. I closed my eyes and took a deep breath, braced myself to go and look for her, but in the end it wasn't necessary; before I could open my eyes Maria had brushed past me on her way upstairs to rescue her. Esteve watched entranced as Father and Tomàs dug the pit, working at the slow, steady pace of ants, and from the back of the house the priest was approaching. I didn't want them to finish digging the hole, I didn't want them to bury Jon and begin to forget him. I took Esteve by the hand and told him we should go before the flames died out and went to sleep beneath the ashes in the hearth. We would have to rekindle the fire. He picked up a stick from the ground and said maybe we didn't need to go far, there were branches right there. I took the stick from him and told him to stop, to quit touching everything and pretending this was his house. I made the decisions around there. Before he could respond, I caught a whiff of the stench he gave off from his eyes all the way down to his thighs; it was overpowering. I didn't want that odour to follow me so that I, too, would be steeped in the smell of dry shit, so I ran. I ran until I reached the slope and stopped in my tracks, you had to descend slowly to avoid falling. Esteve chased after me, he thought it was all a game, but his pea-sized brain didn't expect me to make an abrupt stop and he didn't have time to slow down. The collision gave me a mighty shove. The last thing I remember was a flurry of jolts and bumps, and waking up near the path at the bottom of the slope, covered with scratches and pine needles, snout to the ground like a wild boar.

One of my eyes was covered with moss, but with the other I saw a line of tall trees stretching out before me, and clouds of blue beyond the leaves. The earth under my face was cold and damp. I could feel it, and I could feel the ground vibrate with Esteve's footsteps. He'd been shouting from above, asking me if I was all right, and he didn't stop because I hadn't responded. And just as he was about to reach me, he tripped and fell on top of me. My nose sank deeper into the ground, and though I quickly pulled it out I couldn't stifle a sneeze. I could only breathe through my mouth, if I tried to breathe through my nostrils the smell of death and decaying earth penetrated me, and I wanted to forget everything, I wanted the days to pass quickly, and the benumbing pain to escape to a faraway place.

I rose and saw that Esteve was still lying on the ground like an upturned beetle. I kicked him in the face. I struck him with a branch I'd used to help me stand up, my deadened hand tender, stiffened by pain. Every time I struck his cheek bits of bark broke off. He only burst into tears when I stopped, before that he was too busy trying to defend himself. I'd drawn enough blood already and he was covered with scratches. And all the while he was crying, his nose was running. He wept like a baby, only worse, because he wasn't one. The more I kicked him to make him stop, the more he wept, the more snot oozed from his nose, until finally I took the spoon from his pocket and stuck it in his mouth, and he was quiet. He kept on licking it like it was still caked with dry stew, but this time it was earth and snot.

When we reached the top of the slope Esteve's eyes were red and swollen. Mucus dripped from his nose and he hadn't let go of the spoon. He hadn't said a word. Father and Tomàs had stopped digging and there was no one near the grave. I walked over to it. I said to myself: so this is death, just a hole that carries you off. But before my thoughts could progress, Pere arrived with the pine box. Esteve had disappeared. My brother asked if we should put Jon in the box and then the box in the hole, or should we first lower the box and then dump Jon in it. I said if we put the box in the hole first, and then Jon's body in it, it would weigh less and we would make things easier on ourselves. That sounded good to him. The box only opened on the side with the chicken wire, so we left that face up, otherwise we wouldn't have been able to open it.

The sun was fading, the daylight that was left had an orange tinge. Mother was the first to arrive. A scarf covered most of her face but I knew her eyes were searching for me. The priest appeared, guiding Esteve by the shoulder, his face now washed clean. Then Maria with the little girl on her back. One by one, without a word, we gathered around the open grave. A dry sound broke the silence, we all looked up. Jon's heels had hit the ground as Tomàs dragged him through the front door like an animal pelt. He'd hauled him a few metres when Father appeared with Jon's shoes and gave a shout. Tomàs stopped. Father went over and tried to put them on Jon, but he burst into tears and my brother had to finish the job. The two of them placed Jon on the ground beside the hole, and we immediately realised he wouldn't fit in the box. How shall we do this? Father asked. We cut off his legs, Mother said. Tomàs strode to the stable, slowly but without stopping, and returned with a large saw in his hand. Together he and Father pulled Jon's trousers up to his knees and Tomàs began to saw, but only for a few seconds, he soon stopped and exclaimed: this is revolting. But before the saw had even grazed the flesh, the priest ran off, and leaning against the wall he gripped his belly to keep from vomiting. Maria gave me a kick and told me to see if the man needed anything. But when I reached him, the only thing he said was: you understand me now? You understand? It wasn't rage you saw on my face that day, it wasn't fear. It was shame. Yes. That is what it was. Shame. The only thing a man will not admit to feeling, yet can never shake off, no matter how he tries. And because he refuses to face his shame, he is capable of atrocities, even burying his own son to avoid facing it. Shame. That is all. Understand me now?

2
MARIA

THAT NIGHT, UNDER DARK HOODS AND BY CANDLELIGHT, everyone seemed to have the same face. It was hard to recognise Jon. His face wasn't covered, but when he walked past me he didn't look like himself. And just as I was starting to sense what was different about him, he disappeared into the crowd, and it wasn't until later, when it was all over, that I saw his bloodied hands. I didn't recognise him because he had a pained expression, and I wasn't used to seeing him like that.

He looked tired after the procession. He said I could accompany them to the church, they had to store all the paraphernalia. People were bringing food and the idea was to share it; he'd snatched some of Father's cured sausage. I felt a little shy, but I was keen to go. I said I would if he'd walk me home later, I didn't want to make the return trip alone, that was Mother's only condition before she would allow me to go down to watch him. He said he didn't intend to stay long and he'd be happy to walk back with me, surely I knew he wouldn't leave me alone. But first he had to eat something, or he wouldn't have the strength for the hike to the farmhouse.

He showed me how to wind the rope he'd used during the procession. First you had to coil it around on the ground until the tip was hidden. It was heavy, you had to use both hands to lift it and sling it on your arm like a basket, so it wouldn't come apart on the way to the church. After I finished coiling the rope, another fellow helped Jon lift the wooden Christ that someone had leaned against the fountain. A woman had plucked the thorns and flowers from the statue and placed them in a bundle she carried on her back. The three of them set off and I followed them, me with the rope on my arm and they with that heavy load. I didn't lag behind but I didn't walk too close either. I could hear their laughter without knowing what it was about, and I didn't want to get closer to find out. I liked it there, where I was.

The streets were emptying out, there were fewer and fewer people. Once the procession was over everyone went home. The silence that haunted the village during the procession dissipated, as if a strong wind had carried it off, and all the faces that had looked the same assumed a distinct form. Some greeted me and others pretended not to see me. I was used to it. I did the same. And the truth is I might have blushed if they'd stopped to speak to me. I was embarrassed when someone looked me in the face.

The light from the church made me think of a glowworm in the dark. Outside men chatted and smoked, women laughed. The outlines of the cypress trees rose like smoke from a chimney, stirred by a gentle wind. When we were almost there Jon turned and smiled at me, that calmed me.

He knew I wasn't used to being around people. The men and women who were outside greeted him with enthusiasm, and one of them slapped him on the back. You must be exhausted, my boy! Jon laughed and said, more than tired, he was ravenous. Then one of the women said: that we can fix, and she told him to follow her. He set the statue down and took the rope from me. He held my hand and led me inside. There were lots of people there. And noise. The walls were white and cold. The pews had been arranged along the wall opposite the confessional and were being used as tables; rather than people's behinds now they held platters of cheese and sausages and omelettes. Also jugs of wine. I only knew the people by sight, from the times Mother sent me down to sell leftover vegetables from our garden, and the day she had me pick blackberries on the path to the village to sell door to door. Jon had walked in with me, but soon he started chatting with other men. I stayed in a corner. I felt shy and didn't know what to do with my hands. My eyes started following a pretty little girl who immediately realised I was watching her and started teasing me playfully, making funny faces. I smiled and gave a little wave. She looked well fed. She wore a reddish dress and had soft curls that grazed her neck. With all the noise no one noticed my glances. A tiny bug had slipped under the leg of a pew and was probing the ground for crumbs. I was hungry too but I didn't dare take anything. I was startled when the woman with the little girl clinging to her skirts approached and asked me how I was. Dry white snot was coming out of her nose. Jon noticed that I didn't know how to react and came over. The woman glanced at his hands and told him he better wash them or he'd end up soiling everything. She said I was a young lady now, maybe they'd marry me off soon. She spoke of me as if I wasn't there, as if I'd vanished into those white walls, into that light that illuminated everything. Jon laughed and said I'd marry when I was ready, these things were a woman's business, none of his concern. They all seemed to adore him. The woman gave each of us a piece of *pa amb tomàquet* from a large bowl. The tomato made the bread juicy. I asked her if I could have another piece for later. No need to ask, she said, and she handed me two more slices and went to join a group of women she seemed to get along with well. Better than with me. Jon, too, got caught up in other conversations. I moved the plates that were on the bench with the bug beneath it and I sat down. There was a little crunching sound as the insect died. The girl was still looking at me and she didn't notice. I ate my bread and waited for Jon to tell me he was ready to leave. Olive oil dripped from the bread, glazing my fingers, and from time to time I licked them. Now and again the noise grew louder, then waned and escaped through the church portal. I wanted to leave, I didn't know what to do with myself. Just when I'd made up my mind to ask Jon to go, a blue-eyed man with ashen skin came up to me. He was bald and didn't try to hide it. He said that morning he'd walked to Rieres, the neighbouring village, and found some nice asparagus. One was longer than the pew! He made an omelette with it for his lunch; he didn't have a wife and his daughter was already married, so he'd learnt to make do on his own. He smelled like a caged cat. He said he would never have expected to find me, such a pretty girl, among that crowd. Said he was lonely, his wife, though now dead, hadn't been a good one. Had driven him mad. I looked at him, at the few scraggly hairs that struggled to emerge from his head, and imagined his head also unwilling to emerge from his body. He said again and again that I had lovely freckles, the skin of a lady, white as cream, as if I wasn't made for this earth. I knew he was saying those things to please me, but the more he repeated them the more anguished I became, and the more I wanted to leave, but I didn't know how. The cloistered cat smell was making me nauseated. I was just a girl.

Jon rescued me. I scarcely had time to react when we were already outside and starting up the mountains. The night was cool, the air somehow dense. I had hardly spoken to anyone, but I was happy I'd gone. Jon's hands were clean now. I asked him if they hurt. A little, he said, but he was used to it and it was worth it. For three years he'd been in charge, with the other men, of accompanying the processions, holding the rope taut on either side to keep the crowd from pushing in. What he most liked wasn't the job, but the friends he'd made. They'd always welcomed him warmly. I told him that was as it should be, he had it all, he just didn't realise it. I said if I were the others I'd have welcomed him too, and not just because he was my brother, but because he had that sweetness only children have, but not to get me wrong, he was a man through and through. He smiled, the way he did when he blushed and said nothing, but was pleased with what he was hearing. On the way home I heard so many stories about that group of friends that before I realised it we were almost to the farmhouse. Jon's eyes gleamed in the dark. He was excited, and I could picture everything he was telling me as if God was there, drawing it for me.

That night I had trouble sleeping. It was neither hot nor cold. Jon had passed on his excitement and I couldn't stop imagining what my life would be like if I, too, were part of that world that was filled with people and laughter. The boy was asleep next to me. The stump of his arm peeked out from beneath the bedsheets. He slept on his back and snored in fits and starts, and when the noise stopped I tried to close my eyes, but my emotions didn't abate. The moonlight was blue and bothersome. Sometimes I felt I was asleep, sleeping and thinking at the same time, but I couldn't be sure if I'd been dreaming and had just woken up. When I glanced out the window again it was morning, and an orange light was washing across the sheets.

I got out of bed before the boy had opened his eyes, but he wasn't snoring any more. The floor was cold. When I entered the kitchen, Mother was making breakfast and Tomàs was already in the field with Father. The sound of shovels hitting the earth ricocheted along the walls. There were breadcrumbs on the table, I gathered them up with my hand and put them in my mouth. I wanted to talk, but it was always difficult with Mother. I wanted to tell her how beautiful the previous night had been, and also how distressing. But I couldn't find the words. So I scraped up more crumbs and put them in my mouth and chewed on the ball of paste that was growing larger. I barely made a sound, but Mother knew I was there, behind her. She hadn't said a word, nor would she until the boy came down and she ordered us to milk the cows. He can do it alone, I said. You know your brother only has one arm, she responded. He can manage by himself. Yes, but not as fast, Maria.

It wasn't that hard to muster the courage to ask Mother. I had filled two buckets and the boy had taken the first one back to the farmhouse when Jon came in and told me that, starting next week, I'd be helping the women at the church. They needed more hands. I told him that Mother would never let me go, and he said it had all been arranged. He'd do my chores the days I went to the village. I covered him with kisses. The night before, he'd read the yearning in my eyes. I didn't have to ask him, or even ask myself, if this was what I really wanted. When the day came, I rose earlier than usual to do some of my chores. I didn't want Jon to have to work so hard for me, especially not at a woman's job. I put some lunch in a basket and wrapped a scarf around my head, thanked Jon for the umpteenth time, and headed to the village.

I remember that my finger hurt from chewing on it all the way down, my nerves were on edge, and the parish door squeaked on its hinges. Then all those eyes, those women's eyes, stared at me. Wearied, excited, surprised. The table where they sat painting little plaster angels was covered with stains, and all around there were jars filled with water and liquid emulsions. And saints with missing body parts. At first the smell of varnish wouldn't let me breathe. Then I got used to it. A very old woman rose, pushed her chair aside to make room for me, and sat down again. There was a stack of chairs beside some damaged gilt frames that were propped against a pile of ribbon boxes, and I took one and sat down in the spot the old woman had made for me. I saw they'd already

given me a figurine to paint, a paintbrush and a jar of turpen-
tine, and nearby was the paint palette. I hadn't dared to
speak. But they were women, and they knew who I was and
what I was like. That's why they barely noticed my silence,
none of them had stopped talking, they were soon distracted
and ceased paying attention to me. The angel I was assigned
had a large head and arms attached to the wings; its egg-
shaped hands had little holes in the middle. The old woman
said they were going to make leaves from wire and old
stockings and stuff them in the holes. She went on and on,
stumbling on her words. I painted the face a flesh tone, the
body pink, the hair a yellow colour that reminded me of
wheat. Some of the women painted the dresses sky blue, but
only one, whose name I later learnt was Eulàlia, chose green.
Where have you ever seen a green angel, Eulàlia? Where
have you ever seen an angel, Antònia? Quiet, child, don't you
start. And they all burst out laughing. I examined my tiny
angel, it seemed to be soaking up the paint. It looked increas-
ingly washed out.

When we left, a lot of the women came up to welcome me
to the group, but only one of them truly meant it. Eulàlia was
dark and plump. And bold. I immediately felt drawn to her.
She was the kind of woman who was a bit like a man, she
dared to challenge things and no one ever took her for a
lunatic. Even then I knew I could never be like her. Soon she
became my friend, that was enough for me. I grew very fond
of her, and later I missed her when Mother forbade me to go
down to the village anymore. I couldn't even say goodbye.
But none of this had happened yet, our friendship was just
beginning. She stood out like a bunch of rush broom and I

was tiny like the stem of a daisy, both of us laughed when we were together, and we told each other everything, confided in each other. Apart from my brother Jon, she was the first person in whose presence I felt stronger. But I never told her what happened between me and the priest. I won't say his name, he never allowed me to use it. Father, Maria, just call me Father. Maybe I didn't tell Eulàlia because I was ashamed, he called me a naughty girl, said what we were doing was wrong and we should keep it a secret. I didn't want to disappoint her. But when my stomach started to swell, Mother sat me down and slapped me until I told her who'd put the baby inside me. I couldn't take her blows anymore. That's when Mother went to the village to confront him and locked me up in the house forever. He never came looking for me. For me or our child. I know I did wrong by telling Mother he was the father. They were both angry at me. The priest only came up the mountain when we buried Jon, to bid him farewell, and then we spoke for a moment, in secret. Always in secret. The only time I remember him daring to look at me in public was the day I noticed his gaze following me. It was the first time I'd seen a real man. Eulàlia and I were sitting on the grass threading flowers into wreaths, trying them on and pretending to be queens, princesses, servants. We weren't alone. The women in the parish were there. There were men present too. They were slaughtering rabbits. The village was preparing for a big fête. There'd be rice with rabbit and a dance. Our crowns were the loveliest, because we'd decided to add violets. I was sniffing one when Eulàlia said, Look at that dirty old man, the way he's looking at you! I raised my head and saw the priest. He looked at me for a long time, but I couldn't hold his gaze, I lowered my head. They should hang them all, these stupid priests, and they're fond of saying their minds are always occupied with God, the pigs, Eulàlia muttered. But I liked that he'd noticed me, even if I couldn't remember his face when I got home. I hadn't looked at him long enough.

Afterwards everything happened fast. I surprised myself by searching for him, and whenever my eyes found him his gaze would already be on me. First came the encounters when we were with other people, then we became more daring, then the private assignations. Nothing much happened in the beginning. We met and locked ourselves in that room and I responded to his questions. Especially about my mother. But one day he said the time had come, it was bound to happen and we couldn't wait any longer. I shouldn't be worried either, I wouldn't be punished for what we were about to do, I was just a poor little angel born into disgrace. It had to happen because God had ordained it, everything was decided before I came into this world. He was slowly clearing a table, he said we had to do things right. And then he asked me to sit down and remove my bottoms. And when I'd taken them off and sat down, he put that thing inside me; it hurt at first, but then my groin became numb, and after that it didn't bother me until the following day. I had trouble walking for a week, but I hid it well.

Then I fell in love. I don't know how it happened, because the first times we were alone I was disgusted, he seemed so old to me. It all depended on how I looked at him. Sometimes his falcon eyes bothered me, sometimes I found them attractive. I tried not to see his bald patches. What I do know is that a yearning started to grow inside me, and I wanted to serve him all the time, do things for him, so he wouldn't stop looking at me and finding me beautiful. Always beautiful. I would have left everything for him if he'd come for me and the baby. That's how much I adored him. But I know I made a mistake. It was my fault it all ended. I should've hidden my belly better and then maybe Mother wouldn't have noticed, and he would've wanted me by his side forever. I would've gladly tossed the baby down a ravine if, in return, I could've had him to myself the way I used to, in small doses. I would've taken good care of him, such good good care of him.

3
TOMÀS

FATHER WALKED SLOWLY. I SCREAMED AT HIM LIKE HE WAS
an animal, so he would move faster. If we didn't pick up
speed it would be dark and Dolors would charge us extra for
the room, we'd be letting her know late and she'd have to
prepare the beds in a hurry. We couldn't afford to throw away
money, and I was sure the pine box would cost us an arm
and a leg. If he'd known in advance, Father would have
preferred to make it with his own hands. I would have cut
down the tree. Now we had no choice but to part with our
money.

He stopped at every rock. He was short of breath, he said,
and he pressed his chest with his hands. I reminded him he
was a country man, he should walk and be quiet, like a man.
He said I didn't understand. I couldn't understand, I'd never
been able to. The pain he felt was choking him, cramping his
legs, surging all the way up to his belly. I didn't know what
else to do or what more to tell him to stanch his terrible grief.
I could have gone to the village alone, but he insisted on
coming. And I was getting angry, because I didn't want to be

overcharged. He was getting on my nerves and making me shout at him even more, and then he started weeping in that inane way of his that always seemed fake. His throat produced a series of howls, he sounded like a lost dog, and his red foamy eyes were exasperated when they saw that I wasn't moved and they couldn't hurt me. It should be children who bury their parents, he kept repeating in a low voice. I told him to stop the nonsense, we knew that already. I was sure many men before him had uttered the same words, and the wisest among them had wiped away the tears they shed over their children's graves, realising that it was much easier to beget children than to keep them. They could still engender many more. But still he refused to walk. Deep down I knew what I was doing was wrong, it was an attitude that had fossilised long ago, in childhood, and it was uncalled for in that moment. But I lacked the will and the patience to put up with him.

I sat down beside him during one of his breaks. He was perched on a rock, fiddling with a sharp mulberry branch he'd ripped from a tree a few metres back. Father's mind was clear enough and still retained its powers of perception. Tomàs, you don't understand, he said. And no, I didn't understand. I just wanted to pee. He said I was different as a child, I'd laughed and played with Jon, and he knew we didn't speak to each other now. You can't speak to a dead man, I said. Speaking to a dead man is cheating, it only serves to appease the anguish of the living for allowing the deceased to take to their graves all the truths we refused to hear. For a moment Father's eyes rested on my legs, and then he asked me if I'd killed him. I wasn't angry. I would've done a better job, I said, a man like me who works with his hands, I would've used them to strangle him. He laughed and put an arm around my shoulder. But his laughter turned to tears. And I went off to pee.

When we set off again we could hear the insistent whining of the village dogs in the distance. It was a small settlement, though large enough to have a few animals per household. This had always been hunting country, a land of men descended from men who came from other men who had been born here from time immemorial. No one knew who had laid the first stone. A thousand legends were told, and these found their way into children's fables and the afternoon chatter of women's sewing circles, but none were compelling enough to last. For me it had always been a poor man's land.

Father asked me where I wanted to go first. His moustache was dry and stained with blackberry juice. I couldn't stop looking at it. I say we stop at Dolors's first and then tomorrow we go to Casassas's to look for the pine box. That suited him.

Dolors was the only woman in the region with her own business. There used to be two of them running it, she and her mother, but the elder's passing had only been a carnal farewell, for she had instilled in her daughter her own way of thinking and doing, and the attention needed to ensure that things were done right. But it wasn't just a brothel. There were only a few prostitutes left, and those who remained were more than a bit past their prime. It was a place where men could find respite not only from their wives—and their grown daughters, and the daughters-in-law who had moved in with children and demands and shouting and melodrama—but from the entire female population, except for the prostitutes, who weren't representative of their sex. It was a dump where you felt more comfortable than at home. One of those places that is such a miserable hellhole that, as soon as you enter and see the cast of characters present, you can't help but feel more dignified and pleased with yourself. And it wasn't just the riffraff whose names and lands and sins and drunken sprees you could rattle off one by one. It was that when you fell asleep on a table, your face was stuck to it the following morning, but no one cared if you'd snored or not. The place smelled of boozy sweat and warm beds and fistfights. And it stayed open all night. Sometimes Dolors's son, Esteve, would be asleep when you opened the door, but he'd bolt upright, like he'd just heard a shot go off, and would stand before you hat in hand, with a smile so bright and earnest it seemed fake, as if he could never find the right way to greet you, so he'd stuck with what his mother taught him when he was two years old. He was the village idiot. And not just because the place was a village, but because the wittiest thing some fool had thought to call you as a child was what you were stuck with. And because of that fool, and only because of him, you had to bear that cross, even if only in the memories of those who remained long after you'd left. Esteve really was though. A retard. He was a little older than me, but he moved slowly and didn't think any faster. He was as big as a wardrobe. He had a lot of fat under his chin and on the inside of his thighs, and between his elbow and armpit. His head was small and balding in patches. He went around with a big wooden spoon in his mouth and when he wanted your attention he'd gently poke you with it or stick it under your nose so you'd smell it. It had the most disgusting odour of saliva I'd ever encountered. I still feel like vomiting when I think about it. When his spoon was thoroughly gnawed his mother would snatch it from his mouth so he wouldn't get splinters in his tongue, and he'd cry, and then she'd give him a new one that she'd probably bought from the gypsies who came through now and then on their way from Barcelona. Dolors was his mother. A nicely built female, a formidable woman, with good soft flesh, talkative and intelligent enough so that none of the women liked her and she could bed all their husbands. She was Catalan, but something about her brought to mind the lands of the Spanish south, something in her blood that surfaced when she screamed and swore at you as if she were your mother, never losing her train of thought or her haughtiness. As if with every word, she was adding a silent do-as-I-say, or I-told-you-so. She had large breasts, ashen skin, aged from smoking contraband tobacco. Everyone in the village was familiar with the black, hairy mole between her breasts, because she was the only woman in the region who dared to wear low-cut dresses.

We play just one round today, no? Esteve said when he saw Father coming through the door. There'll be no rounds today. Go and get two rooms ready for us. Ye-e-e-es, Esteve said, and the drawn-out sound hung in the air for a while, and he went about his work. Father strode slowly to the kitchen, dragging his feet, and with one hand he pulled the curtain aside. He didn't have to say anything. Dolors came out, and as if reading his mind she embraced him. She didn't take off her apron. *Bona tarda*, Dolors, mind getting us something to eat? Tomàs, when was the last time you shaved?

I'd already sat at the bar and poured myself a glass of *ratafia*. She had my father sit next to me and came back with two steaming plates of stew and potatoes. I trust this will do, *Senyors*. Then she reappeared with a large slice of bread for each of us. She refilled my glass. I was almost finished and Father hadn't lifted his fork. She took a bottle of wine and started to fill his glass, saying maybe it would be best to tell her what had happened, the whole bit, then he might be able to eat. It should be the children who bury their parents, he said, and he burst into tears again. He made no attempt to hide his despair. I turned around and everyone was staring at us.

That passel of unfeeling vulgar scavengers had their eyes on us, hoping to amuse themselves with our predicament, so they would have something more than drudgery to take home that night. A story to tell their wives when, smelling of fried food, they asked about their day, every wife in the village, all of them as one, indifferent and bland, just as their daughters were indifferent, empty, stuffing their mouths with food without even breathing, waiting for the men to finish recounting every last detail of the story. So the following morning they could retell it over coffee, sitting together in the square on their mid-morning break, while we hauled our pine box from one end of the village to the other before starting up the mountain. The talk would resume the next morning, and they'd laugh at Father because he wasn't man enough to face the fact that death is the only thing one can count on in life. They'd ply themselves with our story as if they were a rich pastry to be consumed in small portions, savoured here and there, now in the wash-houses, now at the far end of town. That's how I saw them, always together, old and young, all of them the same. Hollow. And I didn't want to feed their malice. I grabbed the glass and smashed it against the wall. Father stopped weeping, and more importantly, he stopped talking. Dolors went to get the broom, and as she walked by she smacked the back of my neck so hard it left me dizzy. The men burst out laughing. And in the midst of the ruckus Esteve appeared and said that everything was ready. He'd put us in the same room, but if we wanted two rooms he could arrange it. Dolors said no changes, I had to be kept in check. I finished what was left in Father's glass and snatched the keys from the retard's hands. I grabbed the bottle of ratafia and started upstairs, one step at a time, running the bottle along the panelled walls as I went, that bunch of degenerates watching my every move. I heard Dolors pick up my empty plate and say to my father, What kind of brute did you put on this earth. Better keep an eye on him.

When Father came in I was half asleep. I was exhausted. I only heard the rattle of the key in the lock, the sound of clothes dropping to the floor. I opened my eyes again and it was morning. Father was already up and had removed the sheets. He'd folded them. By the time I came down he was outside chewing tobacco, shoulders stooped, eyes on his feet. He didn't notice that I stuck my head out of the door. Dolors was behind the bar looking sleepy. I poured myself another glass of ratafia and started eating the already cold omelette she'd made for me. I hope you don't take all of this as a condolence gift, she said. I'll pay you for everything, Dolors, it won't break the bank. And while I ate, she waited. She wasn't waiting for me to finish, but for my face to show something I was unable to give, something Father said I'd never been capable of showing. A small movement of my jawline that would indicate I was a person, a real human being. A few tears perhaps. Something to convey that I realised the dead person was my brother. The one who had died was my brother. I knew it was, the one who had died was my brother. But he was dead, so there was no reason to brood. We shouldn't trouble ourselves now. It was over and done, yes, it was all over. There was no point in crying. It made no sense to mourn.

4
FATHER

THINK IT OVER, HE HAD SAID. IN A FEW YEARS, IF WELL-TENDED, all those lands, those fields and paths that came out of nowhere, traversed the forests, encircled Roca Negra and extended further still, they could bring in good money, and they could be mine, have my name on the deed. It was simple. All I had to do was marry. A wife isn't that much work, my father said in a hoarse tone, as if the comment just happened to slip out and he hadn't been thinking about it for hours. It's an opportunity.

I couldn't see his face, but I sensed his zeal, felt his prideful eyes over my shoulder, gauging my weakness. Stop digging, if you don't, you'll grub up the good roots, he said. But I couldn't stop. It hadn't rained for days and the parched earth was breaking my fingernails. My head was more and more bowed, my body bent over the vines, my fingers lower still, but the damn weeds wouldn't come out. I told you to stop. But I couldn't. It should be children who bury their parents. Stop and listen to me, he said again, angrily now. My mouth was full of dirt because the air was thick with dust.

He was standing there, trousers dirty, resting his weight on one leg. As if talking to the wind, he kept returning to the same subject, again and again, while the cluster of roots I was struggling with refused to yield. Damn weeds. It was one of those white-rooted plants that look like bulbs but aren't, with lots of hairy stems, and if you try to pull them out together they're stronger than you, you have to pluck them one by one. First the white ones, then the greener ones. There were also some dry stalks I could've snapped, but the roots were too deep in the earth. It's okay to leave a few, son. You don't need to root out every weed you come across. But that thing put up a fight. I'd been feeling along the base of the plant with my fingertips, ferreting around for stalks, then grasping and pulling the most superficial of the white roots. But the only thing I'd accomplished was to leave some of the plant underground and rip off the top. If only I hadn't stumbled on the shovel that miserable night and broken it in half … It should be children who buried parents.

All that stretch of vineyards belonged to Father. He and I had always worked hard to make them thrive. We couldn't complain, and I saw no need to enlarge our property. Yet he insisted that marrying Anna Planadevall was an opportunity. It was still morning and I hadn't heard about the tragedy of her mother's murder. I'd slept in the village, at Dolors's, and was back at the farmhouse early, when people weren't up and the gossip hadn't had the chance to spread. I knew nothing about Anna, except who her father was, and that she was a feral girl, who lived on the lands where years before my younger brother Felip had lost his way in the fog and never returned. We didn't see him again. Maybe my father urged me to marry her precisely because she was a bit of an animal. An animal plods on without complaining, and would never hang itself from a tree. Now, after Jon's death, after losing my son when it should be children who bury their parents, I can say for certain that my father didn't want for me a weakling like my mother, nor did he want me to turn into a woman, the way he had been forced to after her suicide. He never forgot to put a tablecloth on the dinner table, or change the flowers in the vase he had me place in the centre before any of us were allowed to take that first bite of food, the way she'd always done. But that wasn't why he'd neglected his manliness. It was as if in order to bear the pain of losing Mother, he'd slowly appropriated her through his memories, and somehow by doing what she'd always done he managed to miss her less. Maybe even understand her. I never brought up the idea of his taking another wife. The tears he shed over Mother's body, when I found her hanging from the fig tree and he took her down, made me realise they had loved each other in a way most of us aren't capable of loving. Sometimes I think my father's grief over Felip's disappearance didn't stem from losing him but from the death Mother would always carry with her. She was never the same again. That's why he didn't want me to have a weak wife. The walking wounded were of no use. Only a woman from a certain kind of home can be strong, one where there are no hearts to be broken. I thought that was why he wanted me to marry Anna, as if anticipating events, so if something terrible happened I'd have a strong woman by my side, one who even if shackled to pain by circumstance wouldn't end up taking her own life. Everyone in the village knew who

Anna's father was, and everything she and her mother had endured. Life couldn't have placed more obstacles in their way, or at least few things could be worse than having that son of a bitch beat them.

And I said yes, I'd marry her. He told me that, in return, he'd hire someone to take our photograph after the ceremony. As if we were rich. It would be his wedding gift, a picture of the three of us. My father in collusion, unsmilingly grim beside the woman I'd married, who was skeleton-thin and clutched a tattered sack to her body like a second skin. A sack filled with half-eaten muddy vegetables that had been left on the ground after the miserly banquet that followed the ceremony, and which she'd bent down and gathered. As if she still lived with that beast of a father and had grown accustomed to the idea that starving was the normal state of affairs, the only way to live. But I had married her, and now it was my duty to provide for her, and seed her with children, so she could raise them and together we could make those lands flourish. But the lands I surveyed when I arrived at my new farmhouse seemed deader to me than the dust of my ancestors.

Only one of our children came out wrong. The last one. Since he was born that way we decided not to name him. He had only one hand, a stump on the other side, and he was slow. Anna allowed him to be idle and roam like a dog. I was fine with it. He didn't take much food away from the rest of us; he was often bored and grazed on wild fruits and insects. The others turned out robust. Tomàs was the first. Then came Pere and Jon and the girl, sweet Maria, who later got pregnant and never said by whom. I was fine with that too.

After agreeing to marry a Planadevall, no injury to my reputation could make me fall any lower. I lost no sleep over it. I'm one of those people who doesn't dwell on things once a decision is made. Especially if the decision proves to be a wise one.

The day Jon was killed a part of my heart died. It should be children who bury parents. I stopped being able to feel. It was one thing to lose a brother, a little fellow who was six-year old the day I let him out of my sight while we were playing. It was another matter to lose a son, a young thing of twenty-three that I'd nurtured, made sacrifices for, devoted my time to. Everything I'd done for him had been for nothing. And I came to wish he'd never been born, and I felt selfish and bad, cast aside and forgotten by everyone. Especially by God. I wept like a woman, for many long days and many long nights. I wept for myself, for my mother, for the brother I allowed to run through the Planadevalls' lands on the day the fog took him. I wept so much that a part of me vanished. And I was left with a broken heart. My half-beast of a wife was the one who kept the house going. Tomàs was also strong and did not cry. Pere married and left us. Maria stayed on, but she never again mentioned Jon's name. It should be children who bury their parents. I did not recover.

5
DOLORS

I KNEW SOMETHING HAD HAPPENED WHEN I SAW JAUME COME through the door. It wasn't a habit of his to visit two nights in a row. Or at least he never had before, he didn't feel the need. My mother had just died then. I was still learning how to deal with men, the kind of men I'd have to be around if I intended to put something in my stomach and try to survive. I didn't miss her, but it wouldn't have bothered me if she'd lived another year or two. Maybe during that time, when I most felt her absence, when I clearly needed her, I could have learnt to be consistent, keep my feet on the ground. Not fall in love. But she died too soon, or maybe she never got as far as thinking that one day she'd die and she needed to pass on everything she knew, and I never understood her loneliness, which explains why I ended up falling in love.

That's why, when I saw him for the second time in less than twenty-four hours, a silly smile came over my face, though my mind kept me from rejoicing that he was back, for I was certain something terrible had happened, even if my heart and body didn't quite believe it, and my foolish smile lasted longer than I would have liked. I didn't kiss him. I asked him to sit down. We never kissed before going to bed, at most we hugged. I took a cloth, soaked it in the washbasin and wiped the wooden bar, which at that hour was still dirty from the previous night. I had just woken up and hadn't had my coffee or cleaned the place. I set a glass in front of him and filled it with wine. The same wine I would offer him years later when, with the same sad face, he told me his third-born was dead, some son of a bitch had put a bullet in him. But on that day he had no children. Nor did I. Not even wrinkles. We were still young enough to believe the world would continue as it was. We were innocent enough to think that the history of one's blood was just that: history. Too naive when we trusted that a prostitute's daughter and a land-owner's son could share a life, with the approval not only of others, but also our own. As if any of us, regardless of how much time passed, could forget that our destiny was decided at birth. But, as I said, we were too young, and we would grow up fast. Maybe not that night, but soon, after his wedding or after the birth of his first child, Tomàs, or mine, Esteve, or when we had started to think like adults, both of us, and turned our backs on our dreams.

It wasn't until he finished the glass of wine I'd placed on the bar for him that I dared to ask what had happened. He took my hand without replying, the way he did when he caressed me to let me know he needed to be in bed by my side. I locked the door so no one would come in and make a mess when I wasn't there, and he led me to my room. He undressed me, and I let myself be consumed by love's work, for there are times when we know something is the matter, and it almost certainly won't be good, but we allow ourselves to be trans-ported, we try to prolong the moment of glory, afraid of waking up. When he finished—not me, I couldn't concentrate because I knew Jaume was about to reveal an unspoken calamity—he caressed me, and as he fondled my breasts he said, I'm getting married. It might not be tomorrow or next week, and maybe it won't even be willingly, but I will marry and I know you'll cry, and I'll try not to feel your tears or I might cry as well.

That's how he killed me. Not me, but the little girl that still lived inside me. My past, which now more than ever was only that, the past, was undone in that moment, along with the innocence that had allowed me to see the world in a certain light. Maybe that's when I began to grow up, when I began to love him not as the woman I thought I was, but as the prostitute I really was. I began to love him not as a woman who proudly chooses her bridal linens and attends to the preparations, ensures that everyone will know about the ceremony and that all the unmarried women of the vil-lage will be filled with envy, but as a woman who has grown up and accepted—maybe in this moment her love is stronger than ever—that her love will remain frozen, while another woman steals it from her, snatches away her very will. Or maybe not even her will. Simply her desire, the one thing that keeps the young alive, and when it dies we enter adult-hood, the world of those with knowledge, those who no longer desire but expect things to end, knowing that nothing they wanted as children will come true. That they are too damaged for God to ever bother with a miracle.

When he finished telling me I cried. I turned my back to him, I didn't want to see him or even smell him. The bedsheets were cold, outside the light was beginning to fade. I felt his timid hand on my buttocks, then he squeezed hard; it had always aroused me when he handled me with those large hands of his and squeezed my flesh until it hurt. It was getting late. Nightfall always marked opening time at my establishment, and I was growing impatient. I would have liked to stop time, to be worthy of holding Jaume back and convincing him to stay, as if this had ever been possible. He continued to squeeze my butt-cheeks, both at the same time. He tried to enter me again, and when he did I was too aroused to refuse. I was intoxicated by the thrill of impending mourning, the passion that precedes loss. For a while, pleasure clouded my understanding, but it came to an abrupt end. He continued to moan and grope my buttocks, but my mind wasn't there. Not even my body. It was as if he was merely penetrating my shadow, a fragment of my flesh, imprecise and vague, that held not only me but any woman he might lie with, and the one who would be his to penetrate nightly from then on. Who is she? Tell me who she is, Jaume. I beg you, stop. Tell me who she is.

He stopped and lay motionless for a while. Then he withdrew and sat up. He placed a pillow between his back and the wall. He rubbed his forehead, as if by scratching his head the words might come more easily, the words that seemed hesitant to form her name, lest the attempt make him ill or drive him wild. It's the Planadevall girl. I'm marrying Anna Planadevall. I realised I'd been mistaken. It wasn't the earlier news that killed me, but this, because marrying her, out of all the girls to choose from in the whole of this miserable land, did not mean joy, but pity. I started putting two and two together. Suddenly I remembered the voices of the old women in the market that morning. The story that was the talk of the village that day, and would continue to be until a juicier one came along. Anna, Senyoreta Planadevall, spending the night in the mayor's barn and appearing in his wife's kitchen the following morning, her face still lifeless and sleepy, her unkempt and straw-filled hair gathered with a string, saying: my father, that is, the shameless beast that engendered me, killed my mother some fifteen days ago. She's lying in a pool of water. Could someone help me bury her? Then silence. Or maybe simply saying, My mother's dead and the beast's run off. Is there anything for breakfast? And the mayor's wife, replying, I have eggs. And staring at her. Or maybe, My husband's out hunting. And then falling silent, not because she didn't have anything to add, but because she wished to say something and didn't know how to.

But I went further. In those few seconds I understood why Anna had slept in a stable that wasn't even hers rather than in her own house, as a normal person would if she hadn't been born of a beast and grown accustomed to living like a savage. Anna intended to get to the village by suppertime but was detained along the way, and when she arrived everyone was in bed, only the animals wouldn't be bothered by her presence, for as fast as they wake they are asleep again. So she rested in the hay, perhaps without sleeping, she'd slept enough during the few years she could remember having existed, and she waited for the first light of day, which is so weak in the early hours it could still be called darkness. Or maybe she did sleep, and what woke her was that indolent mayor gathering his rifles and wineskins for the hunt, readying the dogs. She opened her eyes. She was a savage but she was also a woman, and she knew it was best for a woman to deal with another woman, face to face, rather than with a man. So when the mayor left she tied her straw-filled hair with a string and made for the kitchen, where she knew she would find his wife alone. But it doesn't matter. The point is I understood that she wanted to be in the village before dinner, but along the way she lost track of time, because as soon as she realised her father had disappeared she knew she had waited too long already, and now it was time for her to make her own way in life. She had no choice. She knew that marrying was the only way for her to keep the farmhouse and redeem whatever part of herself her father had not poisoned with his blood. And thinking of these things she lost track of time. And while I was in my room sleeping with Jaume and dreaming like a schoolgirl, or more like a baby, that one day we would marry, she had gone to Jaume's father's house and asked that my man, who had never really been mine, be her husband. That was that. Senyor Capdevila agreed, promised her his son's hand before Jaume could even suspect what had happened. And she walked on, hurried to the next stop on her route, which was essential to achieve her purpose. But she arrived too late and the whole village was asleep. The only place she could find to rest—yes, per- haps it was only that, to rest from the fatigue of having lived a life she neither chose nor wanted—was the mayor's stable.

What I didn't understand was why Jaume agreed. Think about it, he said, placing his hand on my buttocks again. It was getting darker, the first customers would arrive soon and I had to get the women moving, they had to start washing and dressing. But I didn't want to get out of bed without knowing his reasons. Our skin was cold. I asked him to lie back down, to embrace me and warm me and tell me why he had chosen her and not another woman. He removed the pillow from behind his back and stretched out beside me. I spread the blanket and curled up so my feet wouldn't hang out. He said: I didn't choose her, and she didn't choose me. I was driven by my past, she by necessity, or maybe it was the other way around. The two things are the same.

I understood. Maybe that was the day I became an adult, at the very least I learnt who I was and what I could allow myself to dream; but he remained in childhood, dwelling in the shadow left by the little brother who went missing on the Planadevalls' lands and was never found again. Jaume was trapped between the guilt of losing his brother and the hope that one day he might still be recovered. Or maybe just the hope of finding his bones. And I forgave him. I was not the spurned woman everyone would think I was had I not been a prostitute, but the compassionate, understanding whore who from that day on would feel only sympathy for him. Nothing more.

So it was pity I felt, rather than pain, when I saw him with his head bowed, on his way to the altar where that wild thing waited, still wearing the dress she'd slept in in the mayor's stable. A dress that was brown like her skin and looked like the husk of a burnt chestnut, and would still last a few more years, until the birth of her third son, Jon, who would later be shot for being more Capdevila than wildling.

But by then some thirty years would have elapsed. My son would be grown, only a few years older than Jon and the same age as Tomàs, just a month and a half apart, the three of them as different as if one embodied heaven, the other purgatory, the last the devil himself. Jon's blood was only a quarter wildling, and this allowed him to understand the world around him, as God would, with no desire to perpetuate brutality. Tomàs, on the other hand, was three-quarter parts wickedness and had inherited from Jaume only the shell, that old-man bearing he'd had since he was twenty, which had fascinated me and kept me awake during long sleepless nights. And Esteve was in the middle, with no known father and no resemblance to me, his mother, because the one quality he possessed could only be attributed to his malady. His goodness was such that he seemed to be there to atone for our sins, and without understanding anything, he understood it all. That's why, thirty years later when Jaume came down the mountain to tell me that Jon was no longer with us, that some bastard had shot him dead, and Esteve asked if he could go with him the following day to bury Jon, he wanted to be by his side, I gave my permission. Jon had been like a brother to him, not a blood brother but a kindred spirit, and Jaume had behaved toward him like a father.

6
PRIEST

WHEN YAHWEH SAW THAT THE WICKEDNESS OF MAN WAS GREAT in the earth, and that every intent of the thoughts of his heart was only evil continually, He was sorry that He had made man on the earth ...

As soon as I reached the dirt esplanade in front of the farmhouse I realised I hadn't come at the right time, not if I wanted to bury him and leave. The men of the house hadn't started digging the hole yet. Maria was there, her skittish eyes glued to the ground, while her scarecrow of a brother, so skinny and shrunken next to her, stared at me with more than just curiosity, as if in that moment, in some foggy recollection, he remembered the day two years before when he found me drenched in sweat and shame and impotence, not knowing where to put my hands. I realised I had left the rectory and mounted the wagon too quickly, almost without thinking where I was headed or how I would begin the eulogy I had been mulling over for such a long time, driven by an irrational wish to use the paltry opportunity God was offering me to atone for my sin, my child. The child that Anna Planadevall, confronting me in my own church, had forced me to keep silent about and renounce, perhaps fearing I would reject it if it happened to survive childbirth. I knew this was my last chance. Either Maria would listen to what I had to say, to my as yet unchosen words, and come what may, or that was the end. I could not pretend I had not had time to compose something, a few well-chosen words. I climbed into the wagon without thinking, and there I spent the longest two hours of my life. It wasn't just the heat, a breeze blew up from time to time and cooled our anguish, though with the wagon jerking about it was hard to tell where it came from. It was the silence that accompanied us the entire way, and the sordid loneliness, despite the two mules and the four people with the coffin, if you could call it that, all of us crammed in the three-seater wagon. There was little water and a lot to say, and we felt the loneliness more keenly than the creaking of the wheels.

It was all so unexpected. The boy came charging into the rectory, shouting and tugging at my cassock, imploring me to follow him: one of the Capdevila boys had been shot. They had killed him and now they had come for the pine box, and I should know this, right? Esteve mouthed silently, as if waiting for an answer I was unable to supply, or reaping amusement from the tragedy, carried away by his own thoughts. Who killed him? It wasn't anyone from the village, was it? I did not know what to say either. These things are not of our doing, though really they are, and I more than anyone should have known.

I took what I could and put it in a canvas sack, strung a cord through it and slung it over my shoulder. A wrapped butter sandwich, a few words for an eulogy, scribbled on a torn piece of paper, but mostly dust, dust that I spread through the room as I paced up and down knocking into furniture, not knowing what else to collect ... Come, Father, come now, we should go. I did not close the church door when Esteve called out again. Let's go, Father, you wouldn't want me to leave without you, would you? I knew the story must have spread through the village well before the dim-witted fellow came to tell me, a churchman was always the last to learn anything around there, news reached me after things had already been avenged, or bought, or exchanged for a wife or land or tools that would be put to use or swapped for newer ones.

It was eleven in the morning. The women had put the soup on to boil, and the rest of the villagers were in the fields, struggling with their exhausted plots and wishing the sun would begin to burn their heads, telling them it was time to put away their tools and eat the meal that had been prepared for them. Esteve and I walked alone through streets that smelled of boiled chicken, potatoes and turnips. For a moment the heat, and the distress, made me forget where I was going. But this respite did not last. I caught a glimpse of them and froze with dread. They had the same stance, the older one more stooped, as if worn down by grief or lacking acuity or discipline. Over there. See them? Esteve's loud nervous footsteps made Tomàs turn his head.

So we're all here now, he said on seeing me. No, we're not, Jaume replied. Jon's gone. But before the friction could escalate, the man who knew them from Dolors's place tried to appease Tomàs. This isn't the time to bring up old family grudges. We must think of the life that's been lost, that's why I have some excellent wooden planks here, so the boy can rest in peace and ... We'll take the cheapest box, just something to make the worms work harder. Well, well, I see we want to prove we're of rough stock, but keep in mind. ...

The one who had quelled the dispute between father and son was Casassas. A stocky fellow, wise as an owl, who thrust his worthless junk on others and got away with setting his price. His eyes, the colour of dry leaves, gleamed with more cunning than usual that day. He was aware that dumping one of his pine boxes on that pair of fools was a challenge, a difficulty to be overcome, if he was to prove he could make the most of any situation. Those two might be stingy, but he was the best salesman in the county, bar none, and it wasn't just his own fastidiousness but also the fear of humiliation that made him want to prove his skill. It was a futile exercise, those people were tough, they were brutes who stopped listening after the second sentence. With them you had to come straight to the point, deal with objects, not ideas.

Quit talking and give me a box, so I can leave, Tomàs said, or you can say goodbye to that silly clasp. No one knew if he was threatening the man, about to knock him down, or referring to the fancy frog fastening on his jacket. Lovely, isn't it? Esteve said. It was garish, out of place in the village, in the whole damn region, for that matter. All right, all right. Now, I know you're going through a difficult time, but we don't have to get carried away, after every storm there's ... But this time Casassas was out of his depth. The stout, well-shaven man who had arrived in the village already married and with his own maid, and opened a shop with too many trinkets, too many colours for that miserable place, still didn't know the ways of the needy mountainfolk. He was a man of the future, not the past, and anyway poverty never features in one's dreams. But I knew how things were, and I was not surprised when Tomàs started to turn away. Why are you leaving? We have our own wood, Jaume said. We've come down because we wanted to make things easier on ourselves, and you aren't helping. You don't know a thing, do you?

What followed, all that business with the coffin, if that thing was worthy of the name, started with that last comment. At that point Casassas had had enough. He could respond with a smile to the threat of a blow, and take the disdain for his frog fastening, but he could not accept an affront to his intelligence. All one had to do was compare the clothes worn by both parties, the layer of soil beneath their fingernails. You can't tell me I don't know a thing. I've proved it over and over. His brow furrowed, his blood boiled with anger. But he was from a good family, he had been taught that a well-chosen caustic remark was more useful than four ugly shouts. So the angry little man bit his tongue, looking like a hot glass bubble about to explode, while the two simpletons slouched unperturbed in the shade, Tomàs chewing tobacco and laughing, as if he had just stepped out for a bit of fresh air.

I have a b-b-b-box, Esteve said, his right eyelid twitching like crazy. Your grandmother's doesn't count, Tomàs responded with his usual agility, the same resolve that made him look twenty-four even as a child, despite his weak muscles and the fuzz that covered his big serious cheeks by the time he was thirteen. Yes—no ... I don't mean that one, it's a different one that's not in the ground. I can give it to you if you want, because it's not mine, is it? It's nobody's. You just have to follow me ... And it took him so long to recall the path there, the secret place or the place where someone had dumped it and he had spotted it, that judging by the length of time he considered the matter, we knew it was nowhere near. And I was right, it was so far above the village, and it took us so long to get there, that I had ample time to consider each and every one of the insults and protests Casassas hurled at us when we turned our backs on him without saying goodbye. This time not even his lofty principles could hold him back.

It was starting to seem that the road and the journey had no end, but silence surely must, for someone would have to speak soon or I would begin spewing nonsense. But then Esteve announced: this is where we turn. He pointed to a path overgrown with weeds that looked like spiky lettuces, a path lined with straw that appeared dead but had always had that thirsty colour. To the left was a dilapidated old villa that already looked like that thirty years before when I arrived in the village, and to the right we could see some wild tomato plants, bits of cracked pottery, and burnt rags. It's at the very end, we turn left just before the mulberry trees and we're there. The poor dullard walked on, with those chubby thighs of his one couldn't stop staring at, and the youthfulness that his lack of understanding preserved intact, despite being almost thirty years old.

Tomàs gave me a nod, inviting me to overtake him and walk behind Esteve. It was a typical gesture of his, not intentional, with just enough edge to keep others in check. Almost there, almost there … Esteve said as he dragged himself down trails no one but him had trod for many seasons. That stupid path circled the entire house. We came across more and more bits of cracked pottery, rubbish, scraps of burnt fabric, and vines that climbed the walls of the house, which were on the point of collapsing. They seemed to have been waiting for us before giving up and joining the surrounding chaos, as if only needing a final nod to succumb peacefully, and yet remain fixed in our memories of that Tuesday morning.

Esteve suddenly stopped, and I kept walking and almost bumped into that sweaty lump of flesh that reeked of illness. This is it. He pointed to something, but his body was blocking my view. So you come here often? No. I come every now and then and sit for an hour or less, and then I go and look for my mother. It's peaceful, isn't it? But in that village everything had an apparent air of calm. You really think it'll do? Tomàs asked. What does it matter, Jaume said, suits me fine. I caught my first glimpse of the thing immediately after Jaume made that stupid comment, that sick thoughtless comment, for no one with any sense, who cared even a little about his son, would have considered using it as a coffin. I couldn't believe my eyes, though it would make sense later. I didn't have to look around in search of an actual coffin, it was clear what they were referring to. I was in the presence of a retard and two Capdevilas.

I stared at Jaume. You wouldn't dare … Shortly thereafter, as if I had not made the comment, I found myself wondering how they had managed to persuade me, how my desire to see her could have been stronger than my convictions. And there I stood, high above the village, backtracking along the path and moving my wagon closer so we could load that thing onto it. Only two men were needed to lift it, and the second of them did not even have to carry the weight, only balance the box, because it was made of plywood, and one side weighed less because there was no wood at all, it was just a bit of wire mesh with a rusty hole in one corner. That abomination that would soon weigh on my conscience was covered in bird droppings, it wasn't a box for the dead but for chickens. It was a small coop, still dirty and festooned with feathers that would remain there forever, for I knew no one would remove them before they placed Jon's body in it. He did not deserve that. He had never been like them, and there was no chance he would have become like them later. That is why I pretended not to see Anna when I arrived at the farmhouse after the long ride up the mountain, with those people that caused me such anguish, and that ball of nerves in my stomach. She was at a window on the middle floor, her sunken eyes looked me over from head to toe, but I asked for Jon, I had to bid him farewell before I could see to anything else.

Mother didn't even close his eyes, said that dark scrawny scarecrow of a little brother, no longer observing me with curiosity but discernment. He remembered who I was. I can see him, can't I? Esteve said as he hurried past me. He had removed his hat and was holding it in both hands, with the fawning politeness of children and the simpleminded, wear-ing the same smile he had on the street that morning, after he came to tell me that Jon was no longer with us. But Jon had never been with us, not really, because in that village, in that deadland, he was an innocent, and he would have still been one if he had lived another year or two, he was a boy who never wished to wake up amid such infamy.

Esteve walked resolutely ahead in search of the dead man, without knowing where to go. The scarecrow chased after him until he caught up, then jumped in front of him. His head was bowed, his legs were crooked, emaciated and bony, as if they might shatter with the next step. He did not raise his head when he reached the door to the farmhouse, and hesitating to enter, he motioned in the direction we were to take. On the right? I asked. He did not reply, but a whimper rose in his throat and he again pointed his finger in the same direction. It was clearly the way.

The house was cold and dark. It smelled of stone and dust. I had to bend down as I entered because the low ceiling sagged. To the left was the kitchen, where Pere stood with a toothpick in his mouth, trying to free something from his molars. He's over there, he said without swallowing the excess saliva. Come, Esteve called to me, I've found him. He doesn't look like himself, does he?

The three of us could scarcely fit in the room. Every time the simpleton spoke, despite the inconsequence of his words, he used all the space around him, he moved his shoulders and swung his arms about, shoving me, and I kept bumping against that greasy wall that was covered with hanging sausages and flies. Esteve did not look sad, he did not seem to understand where we were. You have to be quiet now, I sneered, he was sullying the moment, and his stupidity would not let me think. You know, I've never seen a dead man. I did not respond. No air filtered in through the window in the upper corner of the room, the sky through it was a deep blue, and the light sneaked in furtively, as if searching only for Jon, as if God, having forsaken the rest, had forgiven him. He had the same look of death about him as on the day he appeared at the church three years before, the same pallor of flight and despair, and now he slept the eternal slumber in that musty little room with a dank smell of oblivion.

I thought then that he had come to kill me, that he had found out about his sister and me, so I grabbed the aspergillum from the table to defend myself. But he did not rush in and strike me with his strong sunburned arms, finally relieved from working the fields where his body knew, before his mind ever did, that it never wished to return. He just stood by the entrance in a haze of dust, and he would have looked like a painting, had it not been for the sweat that streamed down his face, and the pulsing of his lungs in his chest. His face was pleading and desperate. He was appealing not to me but to God, or someone to whom he might recount the story I could never repeat, for if I were to talk I risked everything. I could lose my position, the snug comfort I had built over the years with such dedication and patience.

And I saw it clearly. I saw him struggling to remain at the threshold rather than enter, leaning against the wooden portal, as if taking a step back would plunge him into the shame of helplessness and a step forward would extinguish his smile forever. Attempting to remain in that spot, still in puberty, on the road to maturity, green with youth and innocence, yet newly seasoned by the cruelty he had discovered in the world of adults. His face was ugly from weeping, he wore an earth-coloured shirt which had moulded itself to his strong, slender symmetry, as if his body were a David or a sculpture by Phidias.

He has it all and he doesn't know it, Maria always said when she spoke of her brother. And for a moment she would ponder the thought, as if she had never reflected on it before, and then she would utter the words again, so softly that had I not heard them before they would have been unintelligible. He has it all and he doesn't know it. But that day at the church he at least knew that he could stop the evil coursing through his veins, all he needed was courage. Just that, courage.

His beauty had always been an innocence wrapped in fear. His hair was thick and black, his body was stocky, his gaze intense, but his spirit was weak. I had him sit on a pew, guiding him delicately by the elbow, as if I was in the presence of true gentleness, and I went to get him some coffee. When I returned he was still in the same position; his head fell forward limply, his elbows rested on the back of the pew in front of him, his right palm over his eye, propping up his head. I've brought you some coffee, Jon. He didn't want any. He didn't look at me or seem to have anything on his mind other than an image that was assailing him and he wished to dispel. I drank the coffee. Sleep here if you want, I told him afterwards. Yes. Got any tobacco?

He smoked furiously. He had not closed his mouth before he exhaled and was again taking another puff on his cigarette. He had a three-day stubble, and kept moving his jaw from side to side to alleviate the tension, as if he was in a lot of pain from years of worry and helplessness. He was a bundle of nerves. I put him in the cell where I kept old junk: candle stubs in boxes I had never thrown away, books from my youth that I would not read again but no one in the village would use other than for kindling, and the small piano that had belonged to the previous priest, sad and forgotten, with no scores to revive it. A few blankets strewn on the floor served as a mattress, and I left him a sheet to cover up, not because it was cool, for the room was airless, but so he would feel protected. The nights had been stifling for some time, preventing sleep and fostering lurid dreams. Stay today and tomorrow, if you want, as long as you need, I told him. No, I'll leave tomorrow. And the following day he left, taking nothing with him, maybe thinking that he would accumulate possessions later on, as if he still had a lot of living to do, the way we feel when we are young and think everything lies ahead of us, not realising that our lives have already begun to narrow and close, that everything we have lived and thought until then has already defined us, and seldom will anything new shape us in the future. But Jon's journey only lasted three years. He never fully escaped. And when he realised that his had been a jejune evasion, and he would never leave behind the place where life had planted him, he returned to the farmhouse, and there death caught up with him.

Now he inhabited the past again, trapped within the family that had engendered him and doomed him, born only to wither away and purge the banal thinking, the effort required in that household to avoid living as a wretch. Lying in that bed, in that tiny begrimed room, among flies and sausages and jars of preserves, abandoned by all, for had it not been for the two of us the room would have stood empty that morning, he looked nothing like himself, however much I tried to recognise him. Death had stripped Jon of his most valuable attribute, nowhere did I glimpse his long-suffering kindness. Nor did I see the torment derived from having believed the world would not disappoint him, as if everything God propitiated on this earth were molded by His hand, and no one would ever cause harm without good reason. That was Jon, a young man who was too good, trusted others too much, who would have given everything, forgiven anything, had he not had an exalted morality since childhood, a way of contemplating the world as if everything was too beautiful, for when he realised what he had witnessed and with whom he had lived for so long, he could not bear it. Suddenly it was all too much. It takes years to come to terms with certain things, and to reach that point he would have needed space, time to digest what had damaged him, all the things he never imagined could happen. But I knew his mother well, and I wasn't surprised by what he confessed before he disappeared, because, unlike Jon, over the years I had come to expect almost anything from that vulgar brood, to the point that nothing about them unsettled me more than necessary. Everyone must learn to live with their secrets or die for them, they are never forgotten. This was the ultimate reason behind Jon's death, his attempt to forget misfortune rather than accept that things happen as they will, that his inner land-scape had never been what he thought it was, and people always have something to hide. Why else would God have banished humankind from abundance and condemned us to a desert of evil? Jon never recovered. And in that room, even after his soul had fled, he had the same look of fright, of defeat, that had plagued him for more than three years. Not even death could wrest the expression from him. And the whiff of suffocation that exuded from every pore of his body was so evident that even Esteve noticed it, and to mask it he covered Jon's feet with the wrinkled, blood-soiled bedsheet. He did it so gently that I was moved, and feeling I could do no less I drew near and closed Jon's eyes, then his mouth. Then I stepped back and gazed at him, and I felt he was finally able to depart, that God had accepted him into His kingdom, or at least that one last gesture of love had bestowed on him a measure of peace.

Maria wants to know if you would like a bowl of escudella, the boy said, not daring to enter to avoid seeing his brother's dead body again. Lost in my own thoughts, I hadn't heard his footsteps, and now a shiver of fright pulsed through my chest. I had been mulling things over for so long that suddenly reality seemed a mere fabrication. I had eaten my sandwich on the way up, more out of anxiety than hunger, and I told the boy I was fine. I'm-m-m-m ... hungry, Esteve said, and he gave me another shove. C-c-c-can we have some sausage? Those sausages are for selling, came Maria's dry voice. She seemed to have been listening from the other side of the wall, in the shadows at the foot of the stairs, waiting for an opportunity to make one of her triumphant appearances. She had always been quick with her tongue and deft at keeping mum when she should speak. She stepped forward and stood behind the boy, looking at me anew, her face reflected in mine for the first time in almost two years, arms at her waist, hair wild and wavy, the skin under her eyes red from crying. The light that streamed through the front door outlined her frame and gilded her hair, damaged by the mountain air and the heat of the countryside. You go eat something, she told the two simpletons, who hurried to obey her. The first thing I asked was if she knew where her mother was. I think she's asleep in her bedroom. I would like to talk to you, I said in a low voice, drawing closer, as if I did not wish to wake the mistress of the house, although I knew she was not sleeping; she had been expecting me even before I arrived, and when I set foot on the ground she was already at the windowsill, staring me down with her feral eyes to try to frighten me into leaving. Not here, Maria said. She took my hand in hers—how I had longed for that small wounded hand—but she released it at once, and under her spell I followed her outside, then farther away around the house, until I stood before her in the sun. You've grown old, she said. I have always been old. But you seem very old now. And to think you used to look so kindly on me. I look at you as I always have.

She led me there for a reason and I had followed knowingly, but neither of us knew how to begin. Seated on the stone bench, she looked up at me, and with each laboured breath I took she hunched forward. Then she would raise her head again, trying to make me break the silence, which was more hesitant than anguished, for two years had passed since I had spurned her. She busied herself with the holes in the bench, digging away at the grass that had sprouted there, then shaking her hand to remove the dirt. You will ruin your finger-nails, I said. But this time you won't take care of them for me.

She was angry, but she still loved me. I could tell by the tone of her voice, her quiet grace, which did not reflect contempt but an eagerness to please. As we stood in the shade of the house, a cool breeze blew in from the pine forest, filling me with joy. It occurred to me that for the first time that day I was able to breathe. I could see the village, tiny in the distance beyond the harvested fields, I imagined the women crouching and smiling, picking courgette and aubergine for dinner. The road I had travelled up that morning seemed swathed in such joy, and so beautiful in the golden light that heralded evening, that any true notion of how things had occurred would have been instantly dismissed. What are you looking at? Maria asked. The fields, the colours ... You're always in a daze.

In the distance, a steady monotonous thumping. Father and Tomàs are digging the hole, she said, as if she had read my thoughts. On the journey up they had argued over where to bury him. One said it should be under the pine trees, and a long time later, a good half hour later, the other replied that the earth was too damp there and he was too tired to remove heavy soil. He proposed burying Jon elsewhere. After drawn-out deliberations the exchange concluded with reprimands and indecision. I just hoped the job would be done soon. At times one of them pointed out that a certain spot would not do because of the bedrock, or because it was a place of passage, as if treading on Jon would be more degrading than denying him repose by burying him far from the cemetery.

Did it survive? I asked Maria, seeking relief from what had troubled me for so long. It's a girl. And you have not baptised her? Mother will say she's her daughter. Father knows. What he doesn't know is that you put the baby inside me.

Maria was still nursing the child, her dress was tight under her breasts. She said she was planning to leave when the baby no longer needed her, she would not be going far but she would be away for a good while. Tomàs didn't want to marry and Pere already had an intended. There would be a meagre dowry left for her, and her mother had found her a job in another farm that would allow her to put something aside for when she got married. I want … I want to leave, she said in a fragile, penetrating voice that seemed to be begging me to stop her. That's an excellent idea, I said. You will find a good man. Something inside me did not want another man to have her, but I could not make her mine, nor did I wish to. Those years of loneliness had made me reflect on what had happened: the breaking of my vows to God, the apathy that had made me stray from my path for so long, the guilt I felt when passersby looked at me with seeming reproach, without knowing what I was hiding. It was all over now. I had returned to my old life, that of a second-born son who is not the heir, the life my older brother had decided for me. It was not that I agreed to enter the seminary out of love of God, or that such love had, over time, taken root in me more than in my peers. It was simply my lot. That is why I could not be a father, I could never be a father, and though I wanted to see the child, and years later I would refer to her as Marieta, in that moment I did not feel ready to meet her. But the little girl was there, there in the farmhouse, inhaling the same air that suddenly left me breathless, and soon she would awake and begin to cry. I was afraid I would not be able to stop myself from running to her, to console her as I looked into her eyes. I did not know their colour, but I knew they were wide open, there is no bright, healthy infant whose eyes do not seek out the world that is unfolding before them. I was her father, although she would probably never know the truth. Fear and desire battled within me, but neither was strong enough. Maria had been silent for a long time, hurt because what she wanted was to see me angry, for me to take her hands, hold her against my chest, and tell her that no one would ever love her as I had. That I would not let her get away. But that was not what I felt. I pictured myself standing there speechless when she began to sob, but the baby's cries saved me; and here I had believed that no one could resist the cry of one's own child. But I did not respond to my daughter's call. I stood still, wary, feeling like an old man for the first time in my life. I have to go see what's the matter, Maria said. The boy must be busy. She began to walk towards the house, without turning around to see if I was watching, glancing away elegantly, nonchalant and coquettish, offering me a hint of her profile, as if an instinct all women have regardless of age had told her, even before the baby began to cry, that my gaze would follow her. And it was not until she disappeared around the corner of the house that I again heard Jaume and Tomàs's shovels pounding the earth. The grave was half dug.

I walked over to it. In the end they had decided to dig the hole near the vegetable garden, where the earth, still slightly turned after sowing, was easier to remove. From time to time, one of them would lift his pick and smash a rock that refused to yield, or break up hard, dry lumps of dirt that had almost turned into pebbles. They could not both fit inside at the same time. The hole they had dug was the size of the box, neither smaller nor wider: a hole for a chicken coop that was not very big, shorter than Jon but not as fragile as he had been, a box not suited to receive him and bury him, but repurposed to protect him for a short while from the living soil that had engendered him and would soon swallow him. And there I stood, watching as first one, then the other, climbed down and shovelled out dirt. When one of them grew tired, he did not need to say anything, the other offered his hand and pulled him out, and they swapped places and kept digging, until at last Tomàs reckoned that the hole was ready. Jaume held out his hand and Tomàs heaved himself up, one leg out, then the other, using his free hand for purchase. What now? We wait, Tomàs said, and then he added, Maybe we should place a large rock on top when we're done. Wait for what? For the mistress of the house to be ready to bury him. Tomàs began to gather up the tools. Jaume looked exhausted but tried to help. Don't worry, Father, get yourself something to eat. As if his son's words had gone straight into his bloodstream, Jaume swung around and headed for the farmhouse, slowly, without stopping, without questioning where he was going, as if he had forgotten what he was leaving behind in that spot, what the previous night had brought, unconcerned about the coming misfortunes. We all knew this was just the beginning. He was like an animal guided first by hunger, and only then, if need be, by the demands of flock and tradition. Members of a family who in the course of two generations had twice killed a blood relative could only concern themselves with their own sustenance, and only then turn their attention to its source. It wasn't just that they had been culling each other, all children of the same fountainhead, a common ancestor whose name they still remembered, but that they would continue to do so. Not necessarily by shedding more blood—at the time I could name no reason why any of them would commit murder—but by remembering the bloodletting and thus creating a legacy, a family disposition that was not fortuitous, but natural, ingrained. And in the midst of this was my daughter, born never to be recognised by her father or wanted by her mother. And also the boy, the puny simpleton of a little brother, to whom the inescapable legacy would fall when everyone else had died. He would not know what to do with it. Not even then, with his brother lying dead in a tiny, disgusting room inside the farmhouse, did he know how to behave, and he raced through the vegetable patch and the woods, pursued by the village idiot, whom he would soon beat to a pulp.

7
MOTHER

AND ME, THE DAUGHTER HE NEVER TOUCHED, NEVER LOOKED at because he didn't see me as a person, but as an animal, one of the creatures he had more respect for than his own wife. And she, wife and mother, whom he beat but never looked at either, for he didn't even regard her as property to be tended but as a pawn that was needed to produce off-spring. For years he bruised her body, never allowing her to discover the meaning of dignity. He was a beast, a beast of a man, and we depended on him not just financially but also in spirit, and he killed her the moment he married her, and she had me before she realised she was dead. An angry beast who did nothing but grumble and drink cheap spirits, while the fields my grandfather and his father before him had worked—a land coveted by anyone who saw it and had ambition—grew parched and unyielding, defiling the family name that had nourished it with stamina and drudgery.

But a few inherited coins paid for his brandy. A pair of hands made his soup, and younger hands, which I later real-ised would age too quickly, worked his land. But I didn't know it then, I had nothing to compare them with, and it wouldn't have occurred to me to try. I had no time to think, only to work, I didn't begin to have time until I agreed to marry. I was no longer a child then. I had just turned twenty-one. Some will think I took the first chance to marry, or that I married because the only woman I ever exchanged words with was dead—I found her dead and unburied—or because the only man who had given me shelter and sustenance had abandoned me, though without really disappearing, for I encountered him everywhere in the house; the walls, the furniture, even the dust motes bore his name. His grand-father built the house, his mother decorated it, his father had finished paying it off. It was all fruit of the same seed. Some might think I married the first chance I had because I was so wretched, almost as if I were an orphan, though I had parents. I even had trouble speaking, I was a feral creature who communed only with the plough, the dog, and with my mother, when she found the strength to hide her shame and look at me. But no. I married because that was my house, and I expected him, the raging beast, to return one day. I needed to stop and take the time to understand why I would want such a son of a bitch to ever address me again. I recog-nised soon enough that a marriage was a covenant. Jaume wanted the lands my name could give him, the children my womb could offer. And once my womanly duties were ful-filled, I would have all the time God granted me to discover why, each morning when I awoke, my first thought was for the man who became my father at my birth, though I never called him that. All the time in the world to ponder, devise, and embellish the words I would hurl at him when at last he stood in front of me, for I knew he wasn't dead, just as I knew he would return, everyone circles back to the place carelessly assigned to them by God as part of their destiny. If God had paid attention, His bountiful goodness would never have allowed the beast to live, and neither I nor my mother, nor my children, would have paid such a price for his existence. Now my son was dead, while my father had yet to appear at the farmhouse or atone for his sins. Sins that everyone was aware of, more than he ever appeared to be, for these things are not forgotten in such a small village, they travel through the years. I could read it in people's eyes when I went down to shop.

He was a lanky beast. He had never been a well-built man who might have been feared for his strength. But no one wanted to cross him. His legs were long and spindly, and when he bent over it seemed his joints might tear through his skin. His fingers were dirty and yellow, stained from the tobacco he smoked all day, he never stopped to consider whether he bothered anyone with his smoke, maybe he wanted to find out when it would annoy me the most. His waistcoat was so frayed that the colour was indescribable, and he didn't remove it even to sleep or go whoring, though it wasn't dirty, I washed it when he was too drunk to notice me unbuttoning it. With not a trace of baldness, his hair fell across his face thick and stiff, not because it was healthy but because it was full of grime. And his fingers were covered with cuts. Aside from drinking brandy, whoring and beating his wife, he liked to carve wooden figurines.

I remember he was whittling a piece of wood, something long and sharp, and he pointed his knife at me, his hands full of splinters, and said: we have to talk. I remember it clearly because it was the first time the beast addressed me, looked at me with something other than indifference. I was pulling up weeds, had a good handful of them in my hand, and I was so surprised that I dropped them on my knees, and I cried out because for a moment I thought there was a spider, and I was scared of spiders. That's why I never wanted girls, he said, because you're too weak, and then he was quiet. Or he wasn't exactly quiet but he did something I couldn't explain, a gesture he might have learnt from his father or grandfather, an inherited quirk that only looked like a pause, because all of a sudden he added: you`re going to have a brother. And then he really was silent, he picked up the piece of wood and kept on whittling .

That's how he broke the news. He told me because it was the only thing he had ever wanted, and he was so puffed up with God-knows-what sentiment that he needed to tell someone, and apart from the knife I was the only thing at hand. He had wanted an heir, nothing more. I wonder why, because aside from the legacy of his degenerate blood and pompous name, the only thing he could pass on was the ancestral lands his father and grandfather had endeavoured to sustain, to green and fortify against the winter blizzards, and these he was destroying by his drinking and bad character. I was the one who collected him and his liquor bottles from the floor, but it was my mother who reaped his misery. Her face was red, purple, and black when she turned around after my, I'm going to have a brother. He told you? Yes, he told me. For a moment it seemed she was listening to me, but no, my mother never listened. She had responded with a question the way one turns a doorknob when entering a room, quickly and without thinking, an action that is instantly forgotten, and after my reply her eyes focused on something else, and I understood her thoughts had never been for me. She was cooking green beans. That was all we had eaten for days, because I'd grown a lot of them and they were very good. This time I hadn't let them shrivel and grow tough. My hands were still covered with earth, but I wanted to stroke her. Like a wounded animal she recoiled when she saw my hand, the beast had so transformed her that instinctively she feared even her own daughter. He hurt her so often that if I close my eyes now I can barely remember her clean features, her unmarred face. Her eyes were small, her hair shiny and black like mine, nothing like my Maria's red hair, who knows where that came from, a red mane like the devil's. And long. My daughter never wore her hair pulled back. I only saw her with her hair up the day Jon, delirious and caked in blood, lay on the bed where I put him when he returned after a three-year absence. She always was a strong woman, Maria. She changed the water in the basin when it got warm, for Jon had a high fever, but we both knew, though we didn't say so with words, only with our eyes, that we couldn't save him, he was dying. There was a lot of blood and he was growing paler, and he screamed without pain, no longer able to understand his own suffering. My legs hurt too much and I could no longer help him, though if I continued to try, it would be myself I'd be helping. My third born lay dying and I felt no grief. I couldn't understand it. I needed him to live a while longer so I could understand. I was so nervous I didn't notice that my stomach ached from lack of food. Only the baby had been fed, from her mother's breast, and then the boy came and whisked her away. But Jaume was hungry, so he told Maria to set the table. I stayed in the dim light of the room waiting for death to take my son. I stood as still and impassive as the first time God allowed me to observe death up close. I expected it this time, not the first. I had never really contemplated death before then, but after that I began to think about it.

I had just turned twenty-one when my mother was killed, and the previous day my father had told me I was going to have a brother. I had slept little that night, my father's blows and my mother's silences had lasted too long. Despite my exhaustion and the circles under my eyes, I forged ahead. For days I had wanted to set a rabbit trap by a hole beyond Roca Negra. I couldn't eat any more green beans, my body begged for meat. The sun wasn't high yet, so I took off my cap. I liked feeling the wind in my hair, cooling my head. I remember thinking that pregnant women must not eat much, because Mother hadn't come down to breakfast. Nor had the beast. I didn't know if he'd slept at home or if he'd gone down to the brothel late enough to have coffee instead of brandy. The scent of thyme was in the air, I could hear the crickets, and there were lots of snails that I kept stepping on or picking up and tossing among the tall grasses. I walked with my eyes closed, licking my lips, which the sun immediately dried: they went from warm and moist to cool, from cool and moist to dry. Like my thoughts, which fluctuated between two extremes, between life and death. I kept thinking that in a short while I would have a brother, and in even less time I would kill a rabbit— and into the pot.

Without realising it I came to the head of the path that led to Roca Negra. It had poured rain two days before and it was muddy. The path was narrow, cradled by a dense growth of trees that only allowed through a few rays of sun, and the water took a long time to evaporate. There were more snails than ever, and butterflies, and silence. I didn't want to get my clogs wet, so I walked along the edge of the path to avoid the puddles, and when there were none I walked down the middle. The only sound I could hear was the trap I'd been dragging since I left the house, trying to get it dirty because rabbits can sniff out the ropes, and what they need to smell is earth. It was more fun to skirt puddles by walking along the left side of the path, where there was a slope covered in pine needles, with trees and snakes of all kinds, where there was the possibility of falling. I walked on, amusing myself, hopping on one foot or walking sideways, and I almost did fall. I was twenty-one and filled with energy, good reflexes, joy, and soon I wouldn't be alone anymore, soon I would have a brother. I wondered how the beast knew it was a boy and not a girl. I wondered how he knew Mother was carrying a male in her womb, when sometimes he seemed incapable of speaking my name, which was the same as Mother's, after all. I had the same name as the woman he killed when he married her, the one he beat and destroyed for so many years, the same way he had destroyed the lands where I now walked, emptying them of the men who once worked them so he could save a bit of money for his whores.

But I soon stopped thinking about all of this because the day was beautiful, the air warm, and my favourite smell was of damp earth. I knew those lands better than my grandfather and my father's grandfather, it wasn't difficult to find the rabbit hole I'd discovered the last time I was out. It was about fifty paces down a secret path, and no one had covered it up, nothing had changed. I spread out the wire trap and sat down to wait, well concealed and still, because rabbits are fast and clever, or at least I've always thought so because they're so hard to catch.

Not much time had passed when I realised I was thirsty and had no water. I wanted to wait before I went looking for some, but then I remembered that such things as thirst, death and love are inescapable. Sooner or later I would have to go and get some. Maybe I didn't remember this, maybe it was the first time I ever thought it. Font de les Noies was a few steps away. As a child my mother used to take me there, to the Fountain of the Girls, when she was out picking tender fern leaves, which she liked to suck on. I'd pluck off the fern spores and make a yellow paste with water, then I'd bury it. The fountain was very small, a little stone was enough to block it if you stuffed it into the hole in the rocks where the water flowed. Sometimes it smelled of excrement because animals came to drink there; it was a damp place with a lot of puddles, and animals made restless by thirst were drawn to it from afar. I didn't notice the man's footprints when I got there, though I had no trouble recognising them as I left.

Everything smelled as it always had. A scent of damp shade permeated the place, which was girdled by tall thin trees, their light barks mottled with darkness, their leaves overly green. It had the stagnant smell of death that is common where there is too much water, too much life. Various shades of light quivered as the wind blew through the sun-dappled leaves. My mouth watered. I was even thirstier than before, and I would have drunk from the first place I could. But then I saw her. She lay half naked in a pool that was as putrid as she was, and her hair swayed in the water when a frog jumped out as I approached. The rest of her was perfectly still. The water was silty, but every now and then I caught a glimpse of her milky hand at the bottom of the basin, fingers entwined in wild roots. That morsel of death was my mother.

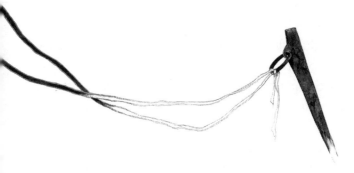

My dead mother in a pool of water, with a splotch on her belly that was a shade of green unlike any I'd ever seen before. An exposed nipple. And her mouth wide open, eyes too, looking up in search of heaven or redemption, serene, as if in that last breath when the beast's face was before her, his cold hairy hands on her slender neck, she had been expecting him, longing for that moment. I grabbed the black woollen cap that was floating in the water and pulled it on like a glove, and I touched her through the fabric. She lay motionless. She was stiff, I could neither drag her nor bend her arms, and the birds sang and I felt no pain, everything was filled with beauty. With her shiny hair floating in the water, she was like a young girl who could finally rest. After all those years of hiding in the pantry, pushing the door with her legs to keep the beast from assaulting her, after all those years of struggling with the beast when he seized her by the hair and shoved her face into the table, she could rest. Strangled and wet. She was all water and earth and spirit, and I was a girl caught up in ineffable contemplation.

I held no thoughts. I made an effort not to think, acted without thinking, the way you would if you were on the run and didn't know where you were headed, but if you stopped to think you'd be too afraid to move. I abandoned the rabbit trap near the hole beyond Roca Negra. I never went back for it. I only took that path once again, not to retrieve the trap but to accompany the mayor and a man I later learnt was a priest. I struggled to make my way back to the farmhouse, though I walked as fast as I could. I didn't enjoy the wind now. The air was hot again, and something in my chest poisoned every breath I took. This time I stepped on the snails on purpose. I no longer cared to eat meat, the only flesh and blood I had ever loved was dead. I decided then that if I could choose, I would never again allow myself to love, because I had been marked by God, and however much I tried to erase death, I carried it within.

That's why I didn't feel sorry for my son, and I didn't give much thought to who shot him, even though he kept shouting, It was him! Who's *him*? It was him, *it was him*. That smell of death, and it was him, *and three men weren't enough to kill the witch*. My son was delirious. Once he was dead there was nothing for me to do in that room. I rose from my chair, hobbled by the painful rheumatism that my grandfather and his father—but not mine—had suffered from treading the lands that my grandfather and his father—but not the beast—had tended and loved and covered with terraced plots and sowed fields. The same lands I traversed that day, aged twenty-one, as I tried and failed to escape from myself and what I had just seen, running toward him without realising it.

No one was there when I reached the farmhouse. I heard the sounds of the earth mixed with the swirling wind that whispered loneliness, and in the distance the chickens, the pig, Father's absence. I was convinced he had killed Mother. The ground where I found her had been disturbed, there were signs of a struggle, and I knew them well; they were the same ones I cleaned up on the nights when the beast came home drunk, looking to harm and then discard the wife he never considered a person. But it wasn't until he told me that he was leaving, fourteen days after I found her dead, that I was certain. Until then I was still waiting for him to offer an explanation.

My eyes were weeping from chopping onions when I sensed he was looking at me. I didn't see him, he was behind me, but I could feel him watching me from the dark threshold. I felt his strength and hatred, the soundless panting that came from his shame. We had lived together eleven days, since he appeared on the third day after he killed her, and still he hadn't had the courage to look at me. Eleven days we had shared the same soup, seated across the table from each other, as he slurped with deafening apathy, with an insolence that wounded me and opened a piercing silence between us. I waited for a word from him but there was only another noisy spoonful, followed by more silence, more waiting. Eleven days passed in this way, and then on the fourteenth day after Mother's murder he spoke the words. Sit down.

I lowered the knife, put down the onion, wiped my hands on my apron. When I turned around he looked greyer and older than ever. I wasn't scared. He had killed her and now he regretted it. It wasn't that he thought he had done anything wrong, but he realised that, after killing her, something that had been his was lost forever. Something was gone and he missed it, in the same way one misses one's money after losing it in a gambling den. I saw in his face that he was consumed with suffering, and for the first time in years not even alcohol could fill that void. He didn't lament being the cause of it, but that Mother wasn't there when he needed her. He had loved her in his own way, just as someone can grow accustomed to a dog's welcome without having to respond, not really noting the dog's presence, save for the day when the animal doesn't come, and one wonders where it is, or if something has happened to it. Yes, in his own way he had loved her enough to choose her among all the women in the county, to have a child with her and try for another. He had sought an heir not only with his body upon her but also with hope, as if having another child, a male offspring, would be the culmination of his destiny, the one thing that would make his staying with her worthwhile. And simply by wishing it he believed it would happen, God would not be so arrogant as to forsake him in this, too. But for years God had turned His back on him, and therefore on the rest of us. No blood flowed for her that month, and it wasn't because Mother had something inside her, she didn't. Her husband had tried to impregnate her, but he had not bothered to fertilise his lands, which yielded less and less. Mother had not bled that month because she had not eaten. That's what the doctor told me a week later, after opening her up, when I said that the beast had not only killed a mother but also a son, my brother. He checked her and said there was nothing there, possibly the lack of food had confused things and made her think she was pregnant. And it occurred to me that maybe the beast had suspected as much, which is why he killed her, because he knew that if God wouldn't give him the heir he wanted, he no longer needed a woman by his side. But I didn't realise this at the time, and I waited for an explanation that was not to come, not even after he told me to sit down.

My beast of a father made the first step, he took a chair and sat, and I did too. He had shaved, but dead skin and despair darkened his cheeks. His eyes avoided me, they stayed on the knife that his fingers clasped and released again and again. I've decided to leave, he said. You'll never see me again. Not even those words were addressed to me. He was speaking to himself, the way you might when something has been weighing on you and you have to spit it out, lest it ends up devouring you. It was for his own peace of mind that he told me. And when he finished, he stabbed the knife into the table and pushed down on it to hoist himself up, because with the amount of alcohol he had imbibed he would need a third foot to avoid falling. I didn't want to help him or see him to the door, and that's how he left, without my touching him one last time, without a word of farewell.

Another day or two, or three, wouldn't make a difference. My mother's body wouldn't care if it rotted away a while longer. I washed my hands and poured out some brandy. I downed it in one gulp. My throat was still burning when I served myself another glass and again swallowed it in one swig. My hands smelled of onion so I washed them again. When they were dry I changed into my mother's best dress and gathered up my hair with a string. In a bag I placed the few coins my mother kept under a step, together with some bread for my supper. I didn't have much time, I wanted to make it to the Capdevila's house before dark. I slipped on my clogs and padlocked the door, something I couldn't remember doing before, but at the time I felt I must, to prevent the beast from changing his mind and returning to impregnate me with the heir Mother had been unable to give him. I needed to lock things up well. He had made my life hell, he had deprived me of my mother, of consolation, even of my youth, for I had been forced to grow up fast. I had tolerated this but I could not forgive. I would never let him control me again. My mother was dead and I no longer had a reason to stay by his side. I had never thought about it before, but now it was clear to me that this desire to protect her was something that had been with me since childhood, an instinct like learning to walk. Never to abandon her, but to tolerate him until she was free and didn't need me, her little girl, in order to go on living. She had done the same for me. She had not taken her own life or abandoned the beast because I was there, I existed, and only when I had been freed would she strive to escape the trap where destiny had put her. She endured despite knowing, with that intuition women have, though we refuse to heed it, that her day of deliverance would never come, or that if it did it would be too late.

I had already fed the chickens and the pig when Father appeared with the news of his departure, there was nothing left for me to do. I wasn't afraid to leave the house or to begin to put my life in order. I set out, not fast but resolutely, down the path that crossed the fields, which grew darker and cooler as night approached, the path that would take me to the village after passing the Capdevila's house. I hadn't remembered to drink any water before I left, and I was feeling the brandy. My tongue was scratchy and rough. I was hungry, but I didn't want to eat the bread in my bag because it would turn into a thick paste in my mouth. I walked faster, tortured by my thirst, harried by the cold. Getting a drink of water was the only thing on my mind. I didn't compose my thoughts or consider what I would say to Senyor Capdevila when I demanded to marry his son. But there was no fountain before I reached the house. When I got there I headed straight to the stables and quenched my thirst at the water trough. A mangy dog appeared and tried to scare me away, the stupid animal kept barking. It was unusual for anyone to pass through that tract of land, and Senyor Capdevila came to see what was happening and found me kneeling in the mud, with my head sunk in the trough. I was thirsty, I told him. Yes, I can see that. And from his pocket he took a slimy cloth and hurled it at me so I could dry my cheeks. It smelled of grease. I coughed, noticed my face flushing. I dried my mouth and stared at him, as if I couldn't believe Senyor Capdevila was standing in front of me. He was nothing like the image I had of him. I had always seen him out riding, and now, in the dark, with his horse penned up beside me, he didn't seem as imposing anymore, whatever gravitas he had was gone. It didn't matter. What are you doing here? I have a proposal. Well then, this is no place for a deal. And as fast as he had appeared, without my hearing a step, he strode out the door and toward the house, expecting me to follow him. I put the greasy cloth in my bag and glanced at my skirt. It was covered with mud, as dirty as the pigs that huddled in a corner, as far from me as possible. I stood up. Senyor Capdevila's spirited black stallion was two heads taller than I was. The animal had not taken his eyes off me since I entered the stable. I had not seen this, for my thirst blinded me, but as I knelt with my head in the trough I heard not only the dog, but also the snorting of the horse as he tried to alert his owner. Now the snorting had stopped. He stared at me, head canted, as if he could read my machinations and with his silence gave his consent.

I jumped over the pigpen, still looking at the horse, and he never averted his eyes. I walked off in silence, making my footsteps light, no stride longer than the other. Just as I shut the gate and bolted the iron bar, the horse gave a resounding neigh. I took it as a good omen; it gave me strength to carry on, not as the girl of twenty-one I appeared to be, but as the woman the beast had punished, forcing choices on her before she was ready. The animal's cry reminded me there was something wild inside me, I sensed the inner strength that had brought me to that point. And driven by this courage, once inside the house, I told Senyor Capdevila I wanted to marry his son. What? Just that, I want to marry him. Can we marry? And he: he's not home now. And me: what does it matter.

8
ROSA

IT WAS A REAL COINCIDENCE. WHO WOULD HAVE THOUGHT I'D have a part in the story my mother told us so many times, and that my father would also share in a moment of weakness. It was a summer morning and the children were playing in the square. My hair was wrapped in a towel, water dripped down my neck. The potatoes were boiling in a pot, and while I waited I used the time to kill ants, one after the other, crushing their little heads, pouring ammonia down any hole where I thought they might nest. My husband wasn't home. The house was quiet, so still it made me sleepy. The sunlight that streamed through the kitchen window warmed the marble countertop, which was scratched and yellowed from all the food I'd chopped. From time to time I stopped killing ants and sat on the stool; without realising it, I would let my thoughts run wild, until finally I would shake off my torpor and resume my task. I had never been like my mother. She always said I wasn't born to be rushed. And I didn't change over time. I understood before anyone else that that was life, just letting things happen. I never envied people who had things to do, desires to fulfil. My husband appeared in my life without my expecting him, the same as the labour pains, the baby girl and then the baby boy. And everything else. When I realised I was gaining weight, I accepted that life was leading me down that path, and little by little I came to love my body again, all new, replete, filled with life. When I had a moment, I would stand naked in front of the mirror and look at myself, I would grip my flesh and imagine I was my husband lusting for me. It aroused me. But what I liked most was to sit on the edge of the bed and fondle my buttocks with both hands and notice how pliant my body fat was, shifting around inside me as if it were alive. Then my hands ceased to be mine and became my husband's; like a dog he mounted me from behind, forcing me to be still and keep my back to him, until he marked me with his fluid, deep in the darkness of the cave, as he called it. I imagined the white fluid oozing between my legs, and by then I had usually climaxed and would resume my housework, dirty and becalmed, content like an animal.

When I realised the potatoes were starting to crack open because I'd boiled them too long, I turned off the cooker and wiped the counter to clean up the remnants of ammonia. Then I mashed the potatoes and the cabbage to make trinxat. The children were still playing in the square, I had a bit of time before I would need to start frying the bacon. I headed to the bedroom, knelt down by the bed, and started touching myself. I was almost there, about to feel my orgasm begin to poison my spirit, when someone knocked on the door. It couldn't be the children, the knocks were from a strong fist, probably a man`s, but it was no one close to me, if it had been someone I knew they would have already opened the door. I stood up and pulled on my knickers. Coming! I jerked the towel from my head and tossed it on the floor, and with my fingers I fluffed my damp tangled hair. Coming, I called out again. I gathered the towel and left it on a chair. Who is it? No reply. Just a shadow, concealed behind those knocks. I said who is it. Let me in, came a raspy old voice. I opened the door. Anna Planadevall's hair wasn't full of straw this time. I noticed because my mother had always dwelt on that detail. Full of straw from spending the night in the stable, she'd say. Yes, you're hearing me right, in the stable, our stable. But that summer morning when she came looking for me, her grey-white hair was gathered up and neat. What do you want? It was him. Who's him? It was him, he killed him, she kept repeating. I invited her in and offered her a chair.

That's why I say it was such a coincidence. Not only because from then on I could claim a role in the story, but because the first time Anna Planadevall appeared at our house was when her mother was killed, and now she was there after her son had been murdered. She was probably not yet sixty, but she looked more than seventy, as if the suffering that showed in her sunken cheeks was calling to her from beyond the grave and she did nothing to resist it. Her eyes were beginning to hollow out and her bones protruded under her skin. Her mouth gave off a nauseating smell, which I tried to temper by offering her a cup of coffee, but that didn't work. Would you like some milk? It's really very good. Bread, I'll have some bread. When I went to cut her a slice, I realised I'd forgotten to wash my hands before I opened the door, and my fingers still smelled of my sex.

She had few teeth left. She softened the bread with saliva, and used her tongue to form moist lumps that she swallowed whole, without chewing. When she'd finished she returned to the subject. It was him. Him, Senyora? Who do you mean? The beast. The beast killed him. And suddenly the old woman's words no longer emerged from her lips but from my mother's, may she rest in peace, trembling words at first, crumpled like a closed-off memory, then becoming more substantial; words that each year, on my birthday, retold the same story. And to think, so big now, and so puny when you arrived, born at seven months; who could have known you'd be born that day, so small, my dear, so very small. And then that crazy woman turns up, half batty she was, and to think she'd slept in the stable that night, yes, in our stable, her hair messy and full of straw. And let me tell you, she looked more like she'd slept in the coop than in the stable, her arms were covered with scratches. Who did the scratching? Who knows, maybe all her life she'd slept in stables, with the animals, all those years she was holed up in that dilapidated house in the highlands, hardly ever coming down to the village, like a wolf made numb to love and compassion. You see, my dear, there was nothing there, she had nothing inside her, those eyes reflected only emptiness. She says to me: it was him. And I say: who's he? She seemed hysterical but really she wasn't, it was just that she didn't know how to behave, so she spoke in a way that made her seem agitated, but in reality she was fine, because when I said I'd help her, well, your father would, she asked for some breakfast and started eating calmly, looking out the window as if nothing had happened. And was she filthy! God knows she was plenty dirty, my dear, and that dreadful smell of hers was hard as the devil to get rid of; it took me a good week to remove the stench, not just from my memory but from the chairs, the kitchen, every nook and cranny where she'd been. I never wanted to set foot in the stable again, at least not until you'd stopped nursing; I told your father that I wanted to keep her misfortune from being passed on to you. And when she told me that her mother had been dead fifteen days and had yet to be buried, I was so upset I almost killed you. I couldn't keep my waters from breaking. See, that's how you were born, with that fright you came out, and look how plump you are now, and here I thought you wouldn't survive, born at only seven months. It's not that I wanted to kill you, love, but I was distressed. A mother suffers, she always does. We spend our lives suffering, sometimes over things that will never happen. And that madwoman didn't just cause me to go into labour, no. I had to get someone to alert your father, the poor man, who was away hunting, so he would find and remove her mother's ruptured, putrid body. But I'll keep quiet on that, your father doesn't want to think about it, and so of course he wasn't there when you arrived, my dear, he couldn't see you the moment you came out because he was dragging a corpse. And there you were, eyes wide open. I swear to you, my dear, that's how you were born, tiny little thing, like a spinning top, but with those eyes that wanted to take in the whole world, and look at you now, how plump you are. Eat up, my dear, eat this *pa de pessic* I've made for you. I know you like it, and you do need your food.

Stuffed with pound cake, I heard the story straight from my mother's lips, and each time it sounded like the feats of an ancestor, one of our dead. And on the few occasions I saw her wandering through the square with her bundle full of things, underselling them for a couple of coins, she looked more like a ghost than a living being. Anna Planadevall —despite her efforts to find a husband and restore the farmhouse, she never rid herself of the beast's surname—was a fable, she represented a story that joined all of us together, everyone in the village who knew her, as part of the same lineage, creating a link that, however weak, gave us a sense of pride, shared spirit, community. And then there was my father, who always looked absent while Mother rejoiced in the misfortunes of others, her gloating obvious from the priestly zeal with which she told the story, the kind where you know what comes next because you've heard it a thousand times, but you can't stop listening. In those moments, Father didn't seem to want to be there, he'd light a cigarette and wait for everyone, aunts, uncles, cousins, to stop relishing another person's misfortunes and show some compassion before he'd utter one of his, Enough now, enough tales of woe on the girl's birthday. My mother had not seen the dead woman's body, which is why she could talk like that, none of the morbid thoughts she put into words came from having borne witness to it. But my father had, that's why he was silent. He couldn't rid himself of the memory of that horror. And when my mother had been dead two years and my father's time was running out, on one of those days when he was in the bathtub and I was washing his old bones, his meagre flesh, he removed his hand from the water and took my arm, so I would stop soaping him and listen without distraction. Daughter, I must ask something of you. I thought he was about to make a confession, close his eyes, and breathe his last. But it was none of that, and he still had a few days left in him. It was more a plea or a reminder. Bury me, above all don't forget to bury me. What are you saying, Father? Of course I will. And that's when he told me, or maybe he didn't so much tell me as get it off his chest, in that moment of weakness when fear, or the memory of it, had grown too heavy. The fear was unspeakable. And it wasn't enough to ask me to bury him, he needed to offer arguments, to make sure I understood why I could not disregard his wishes. He told me the story so slowly that when he finished the bath water was gelid.

It was foggy that day, he said. Very foggy. He could feel the wet grass gradually soaking through his clothes. Large drops of water condensed on the tip of his rifle. He was lying on the ground, concealed behind some bushes, ready to jump up when one of the dogs caught a prey. Father was a good hunter. He charged at the animals with his whole body, never fired from a distance, never killed anything that wouldn't be eaten. He was sleepy, from time to time his eyes closed. The smell of wet iron and the sounds of the awakening forest were intoxicating. But he roused quickly when he heard the unnerving sound of male footsteps, someone calling his name. Enric! Enric! Where are you? Your wife's waters have broken! But before he could get excited they gave him the other news, about the dead woman, he'd have to deal with that before he could be present at my birth. It's not that I didn't want to be there, child. What father wouldn't have preferred, a thousand times over, to see his daughter being born? Or his son, I would have preferred for you to be a boy. Not a girl, a boy. But in all my years as mayor no one had ever killed anyone. I didn't know if I'd arrive in time to put anything to rights, and you weren't in any danger, my child. I would have preferred it, really, but things never go the way we want them to. Things always go wrong.

He said that when he got home, not having caught a single animal, Anna Planadevall was waiting for him, leaning against the large flowerpot by the entrance, the one with the dead tree that still today no one has removed. She was alone, her hair full of tangles and dung and straw. My mother's screams could be heard through the back windows, but Planadevall didn't seem bothered that someone was giving birth so near. But she only appeared untroubled, because when Father approached her she said to him: maybe the child my mother's carrying is still alive. She was pregnant? Just like your wife. Are you sure she's dead? Dead as a doornail. And then Father took her by the shoulders and put her in the wagon, with the rifle and the tools and the dogs, and he didn't stop until they reached the church, and then he grabbed the priest by the neck—he'd just arrived in the village—and he said to him: Come and assist me with this mess or you can forget about my helping you drum up customers. The priest, being quite young, raised no objections, he sat in the back with the Planadevall girl and the rifle and the tools and the dogs, and all three made their way to the farmhouse in search of the dead woman. Father was still in disbelief, he drove the mules hard. He wanted to go as fast as possible in case something could still be done . But when they were just metres away from their destination he realised how pointless it was to whip the animals. Death was inevitable. The fields around the farmhouse lay fallow and dry. The roof had begun to sag in places, the road was full of stones and holes that made it hard on the mules. And when Planadevall told them where to turn, they immediately realised the wagon wouldn't fit, they'd have to carry the dead woman. It was a narrow footpath skirting a deep ravine, and there were lots of puddles because trees kept the sun from entering and dispersing the fog. The mist was thick, as if it were still early morning. The three of them walked close together so they wouldn't get separated. Father said they walked such a long time that they began to suspect they had taken the wrong path. But the smell cleared things up. It was like rotten eggs at first, just a disagreeable odour, but then it grew truly offensive. Father said he couldn't compare it to anything because he'd never encountered such a smell before. We tend to conceal the smell of death before it appears. The sight not only confirmed the fact, it made all of them retch. Everyone but her. He said the dead woman was a throbbing mess of black dust and flies, and worms had begun to devour her. She had been left in a pool of water where dead insects floated on the surface. She was stiff, they couldn't bend her, to lift her out the men each took an arm, the daughter grabbed her legs, so they wouldn't have to drag her. It was a pageant of evil, my girl. God had left her in the shape of a cross, as if she'd been crucified to atone not only for the sins of her killer, but all of our sins. Her face was disfigured, and Anna Planadevall kept repeating that her mother was finally at rest. But she was the one who was at rest. She stared at us the entire way, never lowering her guard, and we were tense, we were doing our best not to vomit on the corpse, trying to be tough like men, and she never complained or cried, she didn't have to hide her disgust because she didn't feel any, she just kept saying that now her mother could rest, water-soaked and at peace. But I saw no serenity there. That was no longer a woman. Not even a dead woman. Just a lump of flesh. A piece of meat devoured by worms, fat worms that left trails behind them, and flies we couldn't shoo away. And that stench, my girl, that stench … even the dogs stopped barking when we flung the body into the wagon, in a sack her daughter found lying on the ground. They stopped barking and cowered. They would have run away if they hadn't been tied up. That's why you have to bury me, it's the only thing I've ever asked for. You understand now why you have to bury me?

Father shouldn't have doubted for a second. I would never let him rot like that. Nevertheless, the next day, so he would die in peace, we went out to buy a coffin and I let him choose the wood. He chose a piece that was blemished, like his aged skin. In just a few months I'd watched him wither away. He didn't have many days left, we both knew it. Slowly all the parts of his body would perish, then the memory of his smell would go, and one day I'd be surprised to realise that I hadn't thought of him for some time. Little by little I would rid myself of his possessions. The rifle would go to my husband, the books I would put away in a cupboard until the children were in school. The study would be shut and locked in such a way that it was no longer part of the house. The same study that years later Anna Planadevall demanded that I open for her. I remember I was nervous that day because my hands smelled of sex. I told her to forget about it, we'd never find the notes she claimed my father had taken about her father, there was too much junk in there and no one had tidied up for years. But she insisted. She said she couldn't read but she'd recognise the papers immediately, I wouldn't even have to help. God would do it right this time. He would help put an end to things once and for all. As if such magic existed.

That's when I realised it was all a game of chess. A game with too many checkmates for one board, and maybe too many pawns, with an enraged queen aiming to topple a king that fate had already forgiven and probably sent to purgatory. I was convinced that the beast she thought had returned to kill her son was not only dead and buried, but that his grave, wherever it was, had already been overlaid by other graves. But she'd spent her life waiting for him, and now she felt him closer than ever. She thought the day of reckoning had come. And she wanted the notes she believed my father had taken after he killed her mother, as they tried to hunt him down. As if by seeing them she could make a clever move, advance a few squares on the board and triumphantly demand an explanation. But it wasn't hard to realise that she'd never find him. And so, led by compassion, not curiosity, I washed my hands and rummaged through the wardrobe drawers until I found the key to the study. Then I opened the door and left Planadevall there while I finished preparing lunch; she turned everything upside down in search of a few notes that, if they even existed, wouldn't be of any help. I felt sorry for her, waiting all those years, not realising that life was that, just letting things flow. And when she emerged from the study with those bookkeeping papers in her dusty hands, believing they had something to do with what she was after, shouting as if she'd just struck gold, I let her be. Mainly I let her leave the house, lest I be moved to pray for her folk and end up praying for us all.

9
ESTEVE

THE PRIEST DIDN'T WANT ME. MY MOTHER WAS DEAD AND THE priest didn't want me. The only thing for me to do was go and look for the boy, he was the only one who ever apologised to me after beating me up. He told me his mother had burned his arm with a candle, the burns and Jon's death and my stench had made him turn violent, and he didn't want to be that way. It was the burns that did it, he said. He even showed them to me. Two blisters. His mother's doing. And mothers don't hurt children, do they? Fathers do. My mother used to say I had many fathers. All those men were my fathers. But they beat her. And she'd scream. Sometimes she only screamed for a short while, because the beating wasn't too bad, or because as they hit her she kept quiet, or because it didn't take long for them to be done with her and leave the room; they would go get drunk and make fun of her while she served them and insulted them. But I didn't just have fathers. I also had sisters. Many sisters. Sisters my fathers beat. And when my mother died, all those women my mother said were like sisters, because they'd always lived with us, they stole everything from her room, everything they could take from the house they took, and I never saw them again. I was left alone and I didn't like it, no I did not. So I went looking for my friend. He was a real friend, he'd only beaten me up once, and he apologised . He hadn't done it again. I knew the way, when Jon died we went up there to bury him. I'd never seen a dead person until then. Neither had the boy, that's why he wanted to take a look at Jon, and that night he went into the room and his mother caught him. What are you doing here? Want to know what death is? You want to know? She grabbed his arm and the hot wax dripped onto his skin, and she forced him to stand the pain. Nothing, she told him, that's what death is. Understand? There's no need to cry, you no longer feel anything when you die. It's when you're alive that you can get burned. Mothers aren't supposed to do that, are they? It's always fathers. My mother's face was always changing, it always looked different because they hit her. And I used to say: does it hurt, Mother? Doesn't it hurt? It hurt when the villagers hit me. She said she only really suffered the first time she had her nose broken. She'd walk by the mirror and couldn't help but look at her altered face, her crooked nose, and then she felt pain, real pain, but it wasn't her nose, it was her heart. The first beating was at the hands of a father she'd refused because he didn't bring any money; she wouldn't allow him to enter her, and to punish her he smashed her face against the wooden bedframe and broke her nose. And though it was really painful she chose to act tough, she let him do it. She only once suffered the shame of allowing it to happen, the first time her nose was broken. Then she got used to it and accepted it.

Like all things in life, she said. Or do you think others live better lives? She learnt to reset her nose while it was still hot and throbbing. That's why I snore, she told me. She'd never snored before. But I only ever knew her with a broken nose, you see. Doesn't it hurt, Mother? Why do you let them do it? She said she preferred that life to having to depend on one man, the way other women did. But it seemed to me she was dependent on everyone, on anyone who came with money in his pocket. Aren't you afraid of them, Mother? They don't love you, Mother. A little love is enough for some of us, we can make it last a lifetime. But Jaume sometimes hit her too. Aren't you afraid of him, Mother? He's the best man I've known. So why is he hitting you? Why won't he take you away from here, Mother?

10
MARIETA

AT FIRST I'D WIPE MOTHER'S FACE AFTER EVERY SPOONFUL, and the puree that dribbled down the bib I tied around her neck, but soon I started waiting until she'd finished her meal because I realised it was all the same to her. Sometimes it took so long for her to finish that the encrusted bits of food around her lips would dry out. I had to dampen the cloth to soften them before cleaning her face, or I'd yank out her moustache hairs and she'd start yelling. It was painful. But at least it no longer disgusted me to touch her, or the things she'd touched. Maybe it was because she could no longer use her hands and I was the one who folded her laundry. She used to fold my clothes, and then I had to wash them again. I couldn't stand her oily skin ruining the dresses and knickers I was supposed to wear. Couldn't stand for her to kiss me. But now she couldn't do that anymore, she could hardly yell or even move her eyes, and I'm not even sure if she still had something inside her that allowed her to think. I never knew if it was a decision she made or just a rapid decline, but one day we found her sitting in that chair in the courtyard and we weren't able to shake her out of that condition. As soon as she opened her eyes in the morning she started with those phlegmy yowls that seemed to last forever, and she didn't let up until she was in that chair. What she wanted wasn't just to sit, but to sit in that chair, in that unsheltered place out in the open, where she could keep an eye on the path that led up to the farmhouse. If we happened to turn her, glassy eyed, to face in another direction, her feeble spitting would resume. I would wrap a large cloth over her head and shoulders so she wouldn't become even stiffer in the sun, and when the shade covered her completely I took it back to the kitchen so I could wipe her face with it in the evening. At first the boy was worried about her, but then he was too busy with the chores she could no longer attend to and he'd never learnt to do before, and little by little he stopped nagging me to take her to the doctor. How will we know if she's dead if you cover her face all day? Esteve asked. Because the rag pulses when she breathes in and out, the boy said. And because of the drooling, no?

Esteve was living with us now. An illness had carried off Grandfather and Dolors, Esteve's mother, and sometime after we'd buried them, Esteve started hanging around the house. Grandmother would come out with a pot full of stones and she would hurl them at him to drive him away. Even when Grandfather was alive she didn't let Esteve play with the boy, he had to run off if he wanted to spend time with him. Mother never said a word. I used to watch the spectacle. Grandmother would try to follow Esteve, her back bent with the weight of the stones. He'd only stop when she couldn't run any more, but then he'd reappear and steal our peppers and cucumbers, anything he could find, never venturing too close to the house, lest he end up perishing at the hands of my grandmother. It was distressing. I didn't want a stone to land on him, so I started leaving a basket of vegetables in a hole near Roca Negra. Grandmother always said she would never go back there. Water wouldn't be a problem, it flowed from the fountain. The first times I returned, the vegetables I'd left for him were rotten and full of flies, so I decided to sing on my way there, so he'd hear me and follow me. Just as I was starting to think that Esteve had left for good or even died, or that the grief of losing his mother had lessened enough to allow him to continue on his way, in search of a place where he could start a new life, I found the basket empty, and deep footprints in the ground. But I still didn't know where he slept, and Grandmother locked the door to the farmhouse at night, so I wasn't able to go looking for him, and with that worry on my mind I couldn't sleep.

And then Grandmother collapsed. I saw Uncle Tomàs running, and Mother shouting with her arms raised, the embroidery hoop in one hand and the needle in the other. Get her off me, get her off! Grandmother was slumped over like she'd been struck by lightning, her lifeless head in Mother's lap, and Uncle yanked her body away from Mother and flung it onto the floor, he slapped Grandmother and burst into tears. It was the first time I'd seen a man cry. Mother got up and tried to hug him, but he pushed her away and she fell down. What do you think you doing, you idiot? I shouted. He looked at me, then turned around and pushed me too, and he started dragging Grandmother's body. He threw it in the wagon we had loaded with ears of corn, and he took her from the farmhouse as if his life depended on it. I had never seen him whip the mules so hard, or those beasts move as fast as they did that day.

It must be true that she's finally kicked the bucket, Mother said a couple of days later when we still hadn't heard from Tomàs. But as soon as she said it, my eyes rested on the horizon, and something was approaching. I say something because first I saw a wheel bouncing along and then a little hand guiding it, and every now and then the wheel tumbled to the ground and raised a lot of dust, and then the little hand lifted it again and set it rolling. The hand belonged to Uncle Pere's young boy. What the devil are you doing here? I asked him. Father told me to bring it to you. Bring what? The wheel. That half charred thing was all that was left of the wagon and the wasted corn that Tomàs had taken two days before. And a bag of coins was all Pere figured he owed us, now that Grandmother's body had been incinerated, as if by offering us that money he was not only easing his conscience at deserting us, but closing that chapter for good. The little boy was my cousin, but I just wanted him to leave. Incinerated? Incinerated? my mother kept repeating to the wind, as if her brain had stopped functioning. But I was wrong. Pere hadn't sent that bag of coins so I'd forgive him for leaving us. He never stopped to consider the harm he'd caused by following his instinct, by being so selfish, and leaving me in charge of folks I only tolerated because I was stuck with them. That money was what he thought the two mules were worth. Where on earth are we supposed to get a couple of mules now? I don't know, Senyora. I'm only doing what my father told me to do, but I believe he gave them to

Casassas, after Tomàs stole his mules. Men, what bastards!

And with no more of Grandmother's stones, no more of that crazy urge of hers to crack open his skull, Esteve was again spotted from the windows of the house. At first he'd vanish like smoke whenever I called to him, but after testing the waters a few times he started coming closer, and soon he was stuffing himself in our kitchen. You'll need to earn your keep like the rest of us, I told him as I shovelled stew onto his plate. S-s-s-í, Senyora. Mother had stopped speaking by then, and I took her silence to mean she agreed that Esteve could stay and live with us. I'm not sure if she never said anything about it because the boy truly didn't bother her, or because with Grandmother's death she'd finally come undone, or simply because she was too busy choosing which damn chair to sit in for whatever time she still had a mind of her own. The truth is I could use another pair of hands, and Esteve was a hard worker. Besides, I was in charge now, because Grandmother was gone and Tomàs hadn't returned, and as for Mother, I don't know that she'd ever decided anything in her whole life. I no longer had to ask anyone's permission. I could do and undo as I wished.

I have to admit I was rather pleased at first. I looked after them and decided for all of them, and it made me feel good about myself. Neither the boy nor Esteve were my children; they couldn't be, not by age, not by blood, and no amount of praying could have made them mine. But I played at being their mother, I scolded and praised them, and they seemed to enjoy it. Some time had passed since Mother had sat herself in that chair, and we barely noticed her presence anymore. Only when we had to clean her after she'd soiled herself, or put her to bed, or give her a few spoonfuls of the mush I made from our leftovers.

It was in one of these moments that I realised I'd hated her for as long as I could remember. It was hard to tell what was the matter with me, because when you've hated someone for so long and those feelings suddenly stop, it seems, at first, as if you can't breathe. As if you've forgotten how to. As if a part of yourself is missing, because that enmity was all-important, though you never understood this, it was all you knew. I'd always lived that way, bemoaning my fate and only thinking of myself in relation to the man who fathered me. Now I was beginning to think I'd been wrong, but I still didn't know in what way, or if I'd ever manage to find out. The important thing was I had realised . My thoughts were taken up with this for a few days. I looked at her and saw her in a different light, but I didn't understand what had changed. I'd find her recumbent in that chair, with her face covered, her legs bruised and bug-bitten, as discoloured as the paving stones in the courtyard, and it no longer troubled me to look at her. I was even beginning to feel sorry for her. But the only thing I realised was that I didn't detest her anymore, I still didn't know why I'd hated her until then. That understanding would come later, when all of this was still nagging at the back of my mind and that disgusting old priest appeared and said he was my father.

I was sixteen years old at the time. That afternoon I had seated my mother on the kitchen bench between two bales of hay, to keep her from falling. It was lunchtime and she was hungry, but she knew I never let her eat in that chair of hers, so she wasn't spitting in protest. I hardly warmed her food because she'd burnt her tongue and the roof of her mouth a few times, and I wanted to keep that from happening again. It took her a long time to swallow, so I used the time between bites to whittle a piece of wood for Esteve to suck on. I'd already warned him that, here, kitchen spoons were used for cooking. He could have that stick or nothing at all. When I thought I'd finished, I ran my finger along the wood to check that it was smooth, and I got a splinter under my fingernail. The damn thing hurt, it was quite far in. I could only get it out by cutting off the piece of nail that was over it. I went to get a sharp knife. But when I opened the drawer my mother began to scream, not spit, but scream like I hadn't heard her scream for a long time. Her eyes bulged, they were dull and red. I turned around and that old man was standing there, scrawny under his muddy cassock, making unintelligible noises. Then he looked at me and his face lit up, and I could finally make something out. Marrrgggta. What? He came into the kitchen and drank some water to clear his throat. He tried again: Marieta. Mother, saucer-eyed, continued to yell, she didn't stop until I wiped her face and untied her bib. He had pulled up a chair. I'd prefer for Maria not to be here, he said as he pointed to Mother. She stays, I replied. And he began to speak.

At first I didn't understand a thing. I suppose he was ashamed to have my mother there while he unspooled the heinous account that he knew would devastate her, that's why he kept going around in circles without coming to the point. He spoke of a corpse full of flies and worms, then about some mayor who'd dragged him up here when he was still young and had never seen evil, but after witnessing that vileness, it became clear. What did? He changed the subject and rambled on, then apologised and said that when Uncle Jon showed up at the church begging for help, it was even clearer. What was? That he'd done the right thing, because all that vileness had to stop. I didn't know what he was talking about but I didn't want to waste more time, I was confused and starting to get angry. I shouldn't have to put up with the sorrowful tales of an old man I didn't know, and who, on top of that, had not wanted anything to do with Esteve after his mother died, he'd shunned him as readily as he'd ordered him to run his errands before that. Esteve himself had told me, all his life that man had treated him like a thing, making him come and go and prance around according to his whims. To make matters worse, my mother was catatonic, in a state I'd never seen her in before, trembling with fear or grief or agitation, and I didn't know what to do, so I told him to speak clearly and stop wasting my time, or get out. I'd hardly finished speaking when my threat made him open up. I'm your father. What? I looked at my mother and her eyes were closed, as if she'd fainted. He didn't care that we didn't want to listen. He went on.

I've only come to see if God's plan, what he commanded of me, has come to fruition, but things are much worse than when I first came here. Everything I did was for nothing. Marieta is living with a cripple and a useless retard, the whole house stinks, the fields aren't tended and everything grows as it pleases, with no order, like weeds; Maria is like a household pet, tied up between two bales of hay without moving, she seems dead, and her face is covered with that glop that looks like goat's vomit, because Marieta hasn't bothered to clean her mouth. She's grown old. God's taken her beauty. There's no redemption. None at all.

He went on and on. I just wanted to be rid of him, and the more nervous I became, the more he repeated a story that was crazy but obviously had meaning for him. He said that some years after Esteve confessed to him that my mother was my grandmother's daughter, he realised it had been a sign. As if God Himself had told him, Take this woman, impregnate her, and punish the offspring for her obsession with rebuilding the family home. He had resigned himself to this role, one cannot go against the Lord, and though he already smelled of old age then, not as he did now but still, he'd taken my mother and planted his seed in her, to put it delicately, and I'd sprung from that. He'd punished my grandmother by raping my mother, because according to him my grandmother never wept for my great-grandmother when a man killed her and left her dead without burial.

Allegedly it was a man. But I know well enough, as everyone does, that Anna Planadevall killed her mother. And someone who loves her mother doesn't leave her to rot in the open for a fortnight, doesn't go back to the kitchen with her hands defiled from handling a rotting corpse without first washing them. That is pure evil. She did not care about anything, she was a wild beast who knew no love. Everyone knows it was evil. It's not just me. I am not crazy. She had such vileness in her that even what I did was of no use, it was all in vain. Look at Marieta. I could not stop that tainted blood from spreading by mixing it with my own. The girl's hair is a mess, her nails are wrecked and bloodied, and she appears never to have worn a pair of shoes. She doesn't understand me and calls me crazy.

I was getting more and more nervous. The man was claiming to be my father. I was repulsed. I sensed his blood within me and it made me want to kill him. Why had he come to me with those explanations? Why, after so many years, had he appeared at that precise moment? But it was easy enough to see. He'd come because he was a coward, he knew he was about to die and was seeking forgiveness. But he didn't deserve forgiveness, he deserved to be tortured. He belonged in hell. He saw that I didn't believe him and could never justify what he'd done to us, so he launched into that blasphemous lie about Uncle Tomàs and Grandmother. He said they'd had an affair. That's what he called it, an affair. Who the hell did he think he was? I grabbed the knife I'd taken from the drawer earlier and I threatened him with it, told him to leave or I'd kill him. He hurried out before he'd even had time to insult me. I locked the door of the farmhouse behind him and began to breathe again. I hadn't realised until then that I needed air. When I returned to the kitchen Mother was weeping. Her skin was red and blotchy, and for the first time I understood why I'd stopped hating her. Her suffering no longer angered me. I'd started to come to terms with things some time before, without being fully aware of it, but now I understood. She wasn't a bad mother. She never wanted to hurt me, not even when she said that she wished she'd closed her legs when I was conceived. But my existence reminded her that the dream she'd taken refuge in wasn't real. The screams and slaps I suffered, the humiliation and worry, had been caused by that man who insulted and violated her, and rather than terror or rage, she'd protected herself by cultivating devotion for him. She couldn't tolerate the idea of such perversity in a man she would have given her life for. My mother had sought refuge in a fantasy, and I appeared and destroyed it. He had no choice but to keep his distance, and she'd spent her life waiting for him. Even after she'd lost her mind and consecrated herself to that chair, she still hoped to see him coming up the road, haloed like a saint. And now he was truly gone. That afternoon we were finally free of him.

11
PERE

HELLFIRE! WHERE THE HELL DID YOU COME FROM? CASASSAS shouted at us. He was scraping Mother's burnt flesh from the charred wood with a shovel, and he stopped to wipe the sweat from his brow. We were removing bits of her flesh from the burned wagons that could no longer be used, and piling them into the buckets Eulàlia had placed nearby. Now and then, a piece of blackened fat oozed from Mother's remains, and we had to be fast with our shovels so it wouldn't end up covered with dirt when we scooped it up. Where the hell did you come from? What was bothering Casassas wasn't that Tomàs had used one of his wagons to build a nice bonfire and cremate his mother, or that he seemed to have done so with the peace of mind of a true miscreant, entering Casassas's house by the back door and stealing his rifle to fire at us. He was furious because Tomàs had purchased from him the paraffin with which to incinerate her and Casassas hadn't been wise to his intentions. The day was hot and dry, all those flies kept pestering them, and drowning themselves in the half-open slimy jars in the shop. And I imagine

Casassas had been busy behind the counter, making sure Tomàs didn't waste his time. Busy calculating how to raise his price without Tomàs realising , as a way of repaying him for his offence more than a decade before, when Jon died and Father and Tomàs left him there, grumbling and humiliating himself in front of the whole village, unable even to sell them a coffin. But Casassas didn't know Tomàs. Besting my dissolute brother was an impossible feat, because Tomàs didn't follow the same logic as others. He had inherited his mother's way of doing things, and the sense to keep his methods to himself. But this wasn't the only reason Casassas couldn't get the best of him. There was more separating the two men than different ways of thinking. An abyss separated them, that's what. So perhaps Casassas's, Where the hell did you come from? was an actual question, rather than just an attempt to keep himself from going insane and accepting the scene as normal. Come to think of it, looking back on that day, Casassas could only recall smiling after he'd sold Tomàs the paraffin, not when he felt the warm coins in his hand, or glimpsed the hint of madness in my brother's face. Pride can blind a man, even a man who knows his pride, because he realises it's not self-regard that makes him seek redress, but the wish to protect himself from the weight of tradition, from the pain of judgement, from the looks of self-righteous fanatics who stroll about intimidating anyone who is unlike them. And yet such a man is careful not to stand out, and he wishes he'd been born with no will, if only to save himself the effort of having to re-press his ideas. Being different brings suffering. And more so if you have to hide your difference, because God placed you here, in this land, and all you really want is to live in peace.

The passel of old women who queued behind my brother that afternoon, eyes fixed on the sale that was taking place, had no trouble recalling that coffin-box fiasco, and they stood for the weight of tradition. Casassas had no doubt about that, just as he knew Tomàs would not escape the web he had spun for him, this time he had trapped him. Years had passed between one event and the other, and God was ready to close that chapter. But Casassas was not quick witted. All he had to do was lift a hairy finger and draw back the curtain that was blocking his view, turn his head, and discover Mother's body in the corn-filled wagon, tossed there by Tomàs. A bit of luck would have sufficed, a gust of wind might have lifted that white curtain and exposed the wagon in the sunlight by the shop door, and he would have realised that my brother had gone stark raving mad. And that trying to overcharge and swindle a madman, who more than a barrel of paraffin that would push him over the edge, was in need of room and board in a penitentiary, was worse for his pride than having shouted profanities and looked like a fool when he failed to sell them that stupid pine box.

I never blamed Tomàs for any of it. I didn't even consider him one of the possible culprits. I always suspected that the bunch of degenerates in my family were all crazy, but it was hard to tell, because sometimes they displayed a certain acumen, and my childish mind latched onto this so I wouldn't always have to be on my guard. A *bon dia* or a *care for some milk*? was enough. I'd try to convince myself that everything my immature and troubled mind had endured had been a fabrication. A passing cloud, nothing more. But then one night one of us killed my brother Jon with a bullet in his stomach. And though I wanted to believe it could have been an outsider, the family's clumsy attempts to cover it up so quickly and move on, no questions asked, only served to corroborate the fact that they, too, had been deceiving themselves their whole lives. The evil I'd struggled to contain, to keep from spilling out into the world, was worse than I thought.

But, no, this wasn't enough to drive me from home. And the bit about the baby inside Eulàlia's belly was still to come. The couple of times she'd tried to convince me to run away with her, I'd refused with a chuckle that proved contagious, we ended up laughing and forgetting the idea, and fucking like rabbits in heat. By then I'd become easy prey for her lust, her brazen ways, even if at first I was rattled by her sudden come-ons. Every time she showed up it was to annoy me, to ask about my sister, wanting to know if she'd ever be allowed down to the village by herself again. That woman did her best to catch me unawares. If the smoke from my cigarette made me squint and rub my eyes a few seconds to stop them from watering, that was enough. I'd open them and she'd be standing there like a statue, with my sister's name on her lips. I told you I don't know, you stupid cow! She'd slap me and spit on me, and then a while later she'd hound me again about Maria's whereabouts, which she was probably starting to guess. But I'd learnt to be careful. I could smell her scent from around the corner, and if I could I changed course. She had the pungent scent of one of those prostitutes who parades triumphantly about, aware that no other female her age could gather so many bees around her grapevine and have the power to scare them away by breathing out one little puff of air. But then one day I slipped up. I'd checked and rechecked every corner of the square, but it was market day and crowded, there were too many animals and spices and vegetables and people with purple-veined legs to notice her sweet, feminine but piquant scent. The sound of chicken feathers being plucked three stalls away distracted me, and I glanced toward the beaked little creature that was scream- ing and doing its best to escape her fate. I turned and there she was. Been avoiding me, eh? Where the hell have you locked up that prissy sister of yours? But this time, after my Leave me alone, you tramp! and her usual slap, she didn't turn away and leave. I did. And that's when her soft, sweaty, plump hand grabbed mine and stopped me in my tracks. I'd never considered whether a hand could be used for anything more basic than grasping the warm handle of a tool or punching some fool in the face, but that hand, supple as a sweet Lenten *bunyol*, made my stomach flutter, and it became indispensable to me, more than anything I'd known before.

Neither being in love nor her constant attempts to have us marry were enough to make me leave my family. I felt I had to look after them, and the closer I was the better, al- though this was a vague loyalty, perhaps passed down through the family and for that reason never fully honoured by any of them, for they all, without exception, had a card up their sleeves. And that was before we found Jon's bloodied body on a pile of earth by the stable, on the point of death and rambling on about two or three men who had failed to kill a witch. It wasn't the only time I'd seen him delirious. One day I was coming out of the pine grove by the farmhouse

and I found him in a state of shock. I asked him who he'd
been in a fight with. He was white as a sheet and didn't seem
to realise he'd sat down on a rock to smoke, and suddenly he
pushed me away with the same hand he was holding his
cigarette with and he set off for the village without saying
goodbye. It took him three years to return, and he hadn't yet
settled into the small room off the pantry where Mother put
him to punish him when, in a manner of speaking, he'd already been bumped off.

I don't know who heard the screams first, but I found
myself out of bed and running barefoot, racing with everyone
else toward those shrieks I never thought could be my
brother's, until someone said, Jon? and I tripped over his
wounded body and fell to the ground beside him, and saw
his face. Then I was no longer running, but slowly dragging
his body, which convulsed as if the ground beneath him was
on fire, and then I lifted his legs and it seemed to calm him.
We laid him on a straw mattress so shabby that I'm sure it
finished him off. It was what Mother told us to do, and no
one contradicted Mother. She ordered us to put him there
with the same coldness with which she sent us all back to
bed. There'd be a lot of work the following day, she said.
What work do you expect them to do tomorrow? Maria
asked. We had already gone to bed, the men of the house
knew it was always best to leave a woman in charge, a woman
like her or any woman who could stand by with advice. It all
happened so fast not even the baby woke up, and once in bed
everything seemed unreal. I kept thinking: Damn, damn ...
Could I have dreamed it? It seems all you have to do is become obsessed with avoiding something, spend your life

fighting it body and soul, and then that thing happens and you realise it couldn't have been any other way ... And still I didn't leave the farmhouse. I needed a more important reason than my brother's murder before I could abandon the task for which I thought God had placed me in that family. I didn't know what kind of sign He would send, but I sensed it wouldn't be long in coming. Then it was daytime. I was still trying to determine whether I'd dreamed up the previous night's violence, for after breakfast we all headed to the fields as if nothing had happened, when Jon breathed his last and Mother emerged from his room with something on her face that looked like a tear. Tomàs and Father decided to go down to the village to look for a pine box.

That's when they quarrelled with Casassas, or insulted him, or maybe it was just that the man felt belittled and the other two couldn't have cared less. The fact remains that they didn't find anything they liked until the following day, when Jon was already stiff and we couldn't fit his legs in the box or position him so he wouldn't have that frightened, agonised look on his face. At noon a wagon that wasn't ours arrived at the farmhouse with a cartload of people. That vulture-faced old priest got out, and I figured he'd come to see if he could make more trouble for us, with that piece of chicken coop they all tried to pass off as a coffin, and I was so beside myself I couldn't stop laughing and thinking: Damn, I might have to accept Eulàlia and get the hell out before I develop a taste for the depravity people thrive on around here, lest I end up needing it like a fish needs water. ... But I was wrong, probably because of our habit of thinking so poorly of the Church, and I realised the priest was there because, like me, he wanted to keep an eye on them. The man had begun to suspect they were all deranged. And he didn't have to spell it out, because when Mother suggested that we saw off Jon's legs so he'd fit in the box and Tomàs was about to start, the priest began to vomit. Fortunately my brother had one of those moments when he was more lucid than Mother, and he said the suggestion was monstrous. But Jon wouldn't fit in the box. The boy said we could break his bones, raise his legs so Tomàs could crush them with a hammer, and once in the box we could bend them. For the first time in his life, Tomàs listened to the poor unfortunate, he put away his saw and returned with the hammer. Father helped me carry Jon to the wall of the house, where the priest was still regurgitating his lunch. We laid him on the ground, face up, feet resting on a stone that jutted from the wall. His cheeks were blanched, his dry mouth kept opening no matter how many times we tried to close it. For heaven's sake, at least cover his face, the priest said, wiping his mouth. I went in search of the black scarf Mother was wearing on her head and I covered Jon's face.

Before he started hammering, Tomàs told Father not to look, or he might start weeping again. But he said it was his duty to look, and Tomàs set to work. I think the first swing was difficult for him, the second too, but by the third his arm fell freely, as if he were pummeling anything but a person. It was a fierce instinct, unstoppable, like a gushing stream that sweeps away everything in its path; he almost ended up crushing every bone in Jon's ankle. Father intervened, he grabbed Tomàs's arm and aimed it toward the other leg, because for a moment Tomàs's determination had us all believing he wasn't bashing in bones but threshing wheat or something similar, that's why we didn't react sooner. But it was a leg, not just any leg; it was our brother's leg. I didn't allow him to wreck his other ankle, after two strikes I was the one who stopped him, pulling the hammer away by the handle. He tried to take it back, and when he succeeded, I pictured myself with a cracked skull. But he hurled the hammer at the tree by the entrance, because he knew that if he didn't, he could have really hurt me. And I thought maybe the day had come when Tomàs had found the strength to contend with his demons. Maybe I could rest now and stop watching over him, because he did have some love inside him, even if it had simply grown out of a need to survive. But the thought had occurred to me rather too quickly, and I immediately disavowed it. I had not yet reached a conclusion when Tomàs started dragging Jon's carcass along the ground, pulling him by the arms toward the hole where the boy and I had placed that ridiculous box. He did so with the cold efficiency he would have used to push a fallen tree out of the way, but at least he had the decorum not to pull him by his crushed ankles. I prayed Jon wouldn't lose a foot on the way.

When Tomàs reached the hole, he straddled the pit and kept moving backwards until Jon's feet hit the bottom; then he began to shake Jon by the upper limbs, like a puppet, until he managed to bend his legs. Slowly he lowered the dead body, which fit snugly inside the chicken coop. We all drew near. The boy closed the wire mesh top, but the priest said it was no use, the holes in the box were so big it was like having no lid. To do things properly we would need to place a piece of wood on top. But Tomàs had begun to shovel dirt, and Jon's tongue and one of his eyes were already caked with it. For God's sake! the priest said. Maria shouted at him that if he was so bothered by how we did things, why had he come with the retard to spend the afternoon at the farmhouse. She was sure no one had asked him to. Listen, I'm no fool! he said. But Mother had approached the pit, and with her foot she started sweeping into the hole the mounds of dirt that had been left along the edges when it was dug. Tomàs helped with the shovel, and we were reduced to silence because the discussion about how to bury Jon was over. Father wept again and the boy went to comfort him, but he must have realised that nothing could console him, and he stepped back. It was clear to me I shouldn't allow myself to get too involved. It made as much sense to bury Jon in a chicken coop as it did to break his bones in order to stuff him in there.

It would make even less sense to cremate Mother's body in front of the whole village, fourteen years later; but no one warned me that Tomàs had come down from the farmhouse and was tearing through the village wreaking havoc until it was too late and Mother was good and charred.

It had turned dark. I was quietly smoking my last cigarette on the bench I'd set up by the entrance a couple of months earlier, and Eulàlia was putting the children to bed. It was my favourite time of day. I'd slowly inhale the cigarette smoke, allowing my lungs to be filled with that deep becalming warmth, then I'd cleanse them with the winter cold. If coming from that farmhouse in the mountains, and spending so many years there, had taught me anything, it was to enjoy solitude. I wasn't like the villagers, who needed to raise hell all day and make a ruckus, and feel like they were being heard. It was enough for me to find myself a quiet, tranquil place. I was lucky to have a father-in-law with enough money to own the lands by our house, and a good barrel of wine always ready to fill my glass, which I sipped by the front door as I awaited the merrymaking that would begin when the men returned from the fields. I'd noticed the smell of a bonfire a while before, but I wasn't bothered. I thought maybe an oil lamp had set fire to a hayloft. That's why it's taking the men so long to come back tonight, I told myself. Damn. I hope the hayloft doesn't belong to anyone I know. It must not be much of a fire though, just a little something that got scorched, and it looks like they've already put it out. And with the repose wrought by fatigue, and my cigarette, and the rough aftertaste of my father-in-law's wine, I used the moment to rest before the crowd of people arrived with their tomfoolery. Every now and then I heard a door closing, or the anxious footsteps of a child whose mother or grandmother had sent looking for one of the men who wasn't back. I continued to smoke and enjoy the moment, the meowing of lurking cats, the sharp cold on my hands and face.

They soon arrived. Like a frenzied mob they ran around shrieking and laughing. I asked what poor devil they were mocking this time. They all fell silent. Parents, children, wives, dogs. And their silence told me the commotion had something to do with my brother. I don't remember tossing out my cigarette, but after pushing through the dark, sweaty mass of people who didn't dare block my way, it was no longer in my hand, as if breathing in the thickening cloud of smoke that was stinking up the village had satisfied my desire for tobacco. I saw the bonfire reflected in the windows before I reached the first house. What have you done, Tomàs? I didn't have time to see anything other than the flaming tongues of the pyre he'd set up in the middle of the empty esplanade before he began shooting at me. You fucking bastard! I headed to Casassas's house and started pounding on the door. Open up, you idiot, open the door! He was already in his nightshirt, Bible in hand. What the hell do you want at this hour? Your rifle. Give it to me! Before he could reply, I'd pushed my way in and encountered an extraordinary family scene. Two kneeling little girls in white gowns, a mother with plaited blond hair praying with them. The lady of the house was so absorbed that only the girls noticed me staring at them from the doorway, their angelic faces turned to look at me, but I didn't have time to say anything because Casassas grabbed me by the scruff of my neck and, shouting at me, he dragged me back to the entrance. If you think you can show up here like this and ... and ... Damnit! I keep the rifles in the stable! But when we got there they were gone, someone had taken them. Tomàs always does things without rhyme or reason, I thought, but later everything makes sense. I was sure he'd stolen them. But Casassas was missing more than his rifles, also the wagon and mules. When I told him it was all my brother's doing, he turned beet red, his obsession with destroying Tomàs raged more violently than the flames in the esplanade. And what the hell did he do with the paraffin? What paraffin? Casassas removed a key from his pocket and opened one of the trunks in the back. He pulled out two more rifles. One for each.

I don't know who took off running first, but when we got to the bonfire Tomàs was shooting and Casassas was firing back. Damn you! Don't kill him, he's my brother! Tell that to the devil when one of his bullets sends you straight to hell! But my brother didn't want to kill us, he was safe, barricaded behind those wagons, behind that thing atop the pyre that we couldn't identify, while we lay unprotected in the muddy grass, with no wall to shelter behind, wearing white shirts that gleamed in the moonlight. If he'd wanted to kill us, he would have done so already. He'd always been a good shot. So despite the heat from the bonfire, the sweat, the distress of knowing that my brother had finally lost his mind, I was at ease, for I was now able to tell myself—it wasn't him. All my life I thought he'd killed Jon, but at last God had sent me a sign. He didn't do it. If he were a murderer, he'd have already killed us, we were an easy target. He didn't want to kill me. He just wanted to be left alone to carry out his plan, and when he had, he'd give himself up to be killed. But I still hadn't realised that his plan was to burn Mother's body. Sometimes the flames hinted at a figure, what might be a silhouette or perhaps a piece of fabric, or hair detached from a skull that suddenly crackled in the turmoil of the bonfire, as if it were a flaming ball of straw. But Casassas's constant bullets and the heat were distracting me, and I stopped wondering what was on the pyre. I didn't really know what I was doing there, contending with a brother I could no longer save, let alone subdue, lying next to a man whose only wish was to kill him in revenge for a petty slight. And then Eulàlia arrived, drenched in sweat and tripping on her dress, smearing it with the mud that kept the flames from escaping the esplanade, and she said that the thing on the pyre was Mother's body. She was winded, she had to stop and take a few deep breaths; when she recovered enough to speak, she told me that earlier that day she'd hurried from the house looking for me, in a foul mood because she suspected I was with the whores who had taken over Dolors's brothel. The villagers informed her that Tomàs had arrived that afternoon, with a two-mule wagon full of maize and Mother's body on top, and that after unloading the body and leaving it on the muddy ground of the esplanade without even a sheet or a blanket, he tied the mules to a tree and left. Some of the villagers walked up to it; the body didn't have an odour yet, and they wanted to know what the thing beside it was: two barrels of paraffin, some said three, but no one put two and two together. They looked on with more curiosity than alarm, for they still didn't suspect the final outcome.

What have you done to my animals, you imbecile? Casassas shouted at him, as if Tomàs could hear. Casassas didn't ask the question again, he realised he had no more bullets left and he snatched my rifle and started firing again. Now and then we caught sight of Tomàs's dark, agitated figure running around the flames, laughing like a madman and firing shots to scare us, and then Eulàlia would start screaming and howling and I would tell her to leave, this was nothing a woman like her should see. But her face wasn't contorted by shock, and I still didn't understand the gravity of the situation. I was used to violence, I wasn't scared. I wondered how the devil that chubby man lying prone beside me could have lost so much in one afternoon without ever suspecting a thing. It was hard to believe no one had heard Tomàs's hammer breaking down the door, or the racket he must have raised removing all those things. But it could well be that those two angel faces, brought up on such pious words, were incapable of suspecting there was evil in this world, and so they watched from the loft, as if it were all for fun, never thinking to tell their parents. Eulàlia kept talking and repeating what she'd been told, as if she needed to keep her mind occupied, fearing to open her eyes and discover it was all true. I thought it didn't matter what they'd said, the important thing now was not what had happened, but how we could fix things so my brother wouldn't end up with a bullet in his head, and the family with another violent death on our hands. Besides, I was convinced the people who were gathered on the esplanade hadn't paid that much attention as they watched Tomàs stack one wagon on the other, then lay Mother's body on top and douse it with paraffin. You couldn't trust what the villagers said. They'd congregated there to rest from the fatigue of working the fields, they had looked on in a daze, excited by the story they'd tell their wives as they apologised for delaying their sweaty return; they knew that with all the commotion, there would be no punishment or recrimination that night. That's why, when evening came and their bellies began to rumble, they abandoned Tomàs and his infernal designs and headed home, to the tables their wives had set for them, reappearing only at first light, to again neglect their fields. We were worn out by then. All night we'd been up against an enemy who should not have been one, who seemed to have an unending supply of fuel for the bonfire.

At dawn I saw the staring faces of the people who stood there without lifting a finger to help, and Eulàlia's contorted expression, not just from lack of sleep. She continued to talk as if deranged, repeating again and again the story she'd been told by the villagers the previous day. She seemed to be talking to herself, and as soon as she finished she would start again, as if her memory sought to protect her by erasing from her mind the moment Tomàs lit the match and tossed it on the pyre. I couldn't take my eyes off her. I was worried about her. When I'd made up my mind to say something, or maybe hug her and give her a kiss, a sharp blow from Casassas made me raise my head. And I saw that nothing was left of the mound but a charred, dishonoured body, some burnt wood, a few flames still flickering. Tomàs was walking away and no one followed him. I didn't want to go after him. I had to stay with Eulàlia. She wasn't ready for that, she didn't deserve any of it. She would never leave me, but I feared she'd finally grasped the depravity of my kin. It was one thing to say she understood me, to hug me and promise she'd always be by my side, it was quite another to have been forced to witness such a scene.

After we'd buried Jon and Eulàlia told me she was pregnant, I thought God had set me the task of preventing more wickedness from being born into my family. I thought I was leaving my home to become a man, not just to escape that place. I knew the priest was watching them and wouldn't need much help to surveil that pack of fools, so I felt I could leave and marry Eulàlia. But my first child was almost a year old and I still thought I needed to be vigilant. I looked at my boy in the too-small highchair that my father-in-law built for him, watched him gulp the food Eulàlia stuffed in his mouth, and I thought: He licks just like Mother, he sops his bread the way she did. This was on my mind for days, and when Eulàlia fed him I couldn't help but walk over and stare, until one day she noticed me on the other side of the window. She turned to look at me and said: what on earth are you doing planted there like a tree? I told her and she laughed. How else was the child supposed to eat, without any teeth? I realised she was right, maybe my family's blood hadn't ruined the child after all. Time passed, days and months and years, and I grew calmer. I wasn't always on my guard. I noticed I laughed more often, and with Eulàlia by my side I began to take a liking to life. Maybe, just maybe, I had been saved, she had saved me. Now I couldn't disappoint her. Not after she had saved me. I couldn't shatter all that goodness. So I asked God to stop saddling me with all the burdens I could withstand.

12
JON

FIRST CAME THE SHOT AND THEN DEATH. OR FIRST THE SHOT and then the suffering that led to my death. But above all, death. In the early days there was confusion, not only because it seemed even the living didn't know who killed me, but because I didn't remember it either. It was as if my non-body had forgotten what I had experienced because my mind was too preoccupied debating whether to leave non-death and enter non-life. I still had ears when I was buried, I heard the specks of earth coming down on me, dusting my mouth, then someone weeping, and later the weight of oblivion interring me. Then it was dark, my non-body realised I was more and more dead. It was inevitable, maybe it always had been. Maybe there never was a truce between me and my brother, and I was the only person naive enough to think that one day there might be a solution. It's entirely possible, or at least not inconceivable, that on the day I found Tomàs on that bend in the stream, forcing himself on Mother, our mother, he had already made up his mind to shoot me in the back. Like an animal.

I'd been looking for the boy a long time that morning. Pere and I had picked some large tomatoes that we'd been watering for days, and I was sure the boy would want to be the first to try them. The heady scent of tomato filled the air. The boy wasn't in the kitchen or his room, so I decided to look around; sometimes he built a hut in one of the clearings. I didn't call to him because I didn't want Tomàs to see that I wasn't working. Besides, he didn't like us talking to the little fellow, even though he was our brother. I always thought Tomàs didn't consider him a real man because Mother had never put him to work. But the truth is the boy had turned out puny and strange, and he seemed too weak for the adult world. One of his arms never grew properly, and he was left with something that resembled a small, crooked, spongy sort of an eagle's beak. But it only looked soft. He let me touch it once and it wasn't soft inside, there was a good handful of bones in there, the problem was they were all in a jumble, heaped together rather than stretched out. Aside from wanting to give him the tomato, that morning I was worried about him because it was brutally hot and I was afraid he'd faint. It had happened before. Breathing that air was like swallowing fireballs. Even the tomato in my hand was beginning to soften, soaked in a sticky kind of sweat.

I'd been looking for him for a good while when I heard some animal-like snorts. I stood motionless, I'd never heard such sounds before. The panting got louder the closer I drew to the bend, and after each huff and puff came the sound of someone striking an animal. Hard, dry blows, as if from a flat hand on skin. If someone had told me what I would see when I lowered my eyes to the bend in the stream, I would have stepped back without hesitating. But no one warned me. At least not in that moment, and never clearly, though the priest had told me again and again. That's why we were cast out of paradise, and why Yahweh lamented having placed man on earth. But until then the priest's stories belonged to the remote past. I hadn't realised that the man in the scriptures was all of us, we all descended from him. My brother more so than others, because that crazed panting wasn't an animal, it was Tomàs. He was behind Mother, thrusting like a bull, while she clung with both hands to the exposed roots along the wild, sandy banks of the stream. She was grunting like a cow, and he slapped her buttocks, beneath her raised skirt; the harder he hit her the more he salivated. I couldn't see their faces because they had their backs to me, but from time to time I could hear Tomàs swallowing the saliva in his mouth. With his free hand, he pushed Mother's head into the crumbling earth beneath the roots; she seemed to be having trouble breathing, her cries came out dirty, mixed with dust. He kept saying she was his. And she responded, yes, his forever, and he slapped and slapped until finally he stopped. I couldn't move. I would have liked to run away so I could stop looking at them, but a part of me didn't believe what I saw and needed to stay longer in order to digest it, not just with my eyes but also with my mind. When the violence ended, her face still sunk in the ground, her buttocks up, he started stroking her gently, tracing the line of her back with his fingertips. She said nothing, as if suddenly she loved him. A fierce, murderous instinct grew in me, an anger I'd never felt before, and I tried to contain it, I wanted to keep it from seeping out, and it stayed in my throat. I wanted to kill my brother, drown him. But that wasn't me. I didn't want that to be me. I'd never been like that, and I couldn't kill him because he was my brother. But she was my mother. It was all too much for me. I took the tomato that was disintegrating in my hand, because I'd squeezed it, and hurled it at Tomàs. Then I started running and didn't stop, not even when I fell and my arm and leg started bleeding. I didn't stop until I reached the pine forest at Font de les Noies and there I began to shout. Very loudly. I shouted because the pain was unbearable and anger choked my thoughts. I needed to rid myself of it, rip it out. I wept too, not from pain, but helplessness. What angered me most was that the sin could have been avoided, it had been a decision, not the result of randomness, like a storm or a grapevine disease. That while my father, that spineless man who did nothing but work, who seemed to have little else inside him other than his love of the land, strove to raise his family, his heir had decided to take his wife whenever he felt the need to satisfy himself. His heir, his own son, grabbing his mother as if she were a thing, slapping her buttocks until they were red.

That is why, my son, Yahweh regretted making man on earth, the priest repeated with neither surprise nor sorrow, almost as if he'd been expecting the confession I made when I came into the church that day. I was still sweating, anguished, my legs wanted to keep running, but my thoughts had settled a bit. I wasn't seeking consolation, perhaps just a bit of time to think about what came next. That night, as rage kept me from sleep, I decided to run away and try to forgive. Maybe even forget. But a time came when I realised it was useless to keep running, because that thing was inside me. A man must face things. Three years were enough to give Tomàs the chance to repent and put a stop to the barbarism. And so I returned. Thinking, perhaps, that this time I would have the courage to kill the man or brother or wild bull who had dishonoured his own mother in such a terrible way, and at the same time knowing that I would never have the guts to do so, that I was only returning so he could swear to me that it was all over. That it had only happened that one time. It had been a moment of weakness such as any man could have, an interlude from the heavy burden of morality. But no, he had no intention of stopping. I pointed my shotgun at him and gave him one last chance. All he had to do was say it was over. I told him I didn't care what he'd been up to with Mother while I'd been gone, but in return he had to agree that, now, it was over. No, Jon, he said calmly. I won't stop. You don't understand. You will never understand us.

I had only one option left, it was clear to me then. The time had come to fire my gun. He stood still, calm, chewing tobacco, resting against a pile of straw on what would be my last night, without changing his mind and without trying to stop me. My trembling hands took aim, I tried to summon the courage to kill him. But I couldn't do it. Rather than the divine seal, I chose flight. My mistake wasn't that I spared his life, but that I dropped the shotgun on the ground before fleeing again. He grabbed it and shot me from behind, like an animal. One shot and then death. Or first a shot and then the pain that led to my death. But above all death.

13
ENRIQUETA

I TRIED NOT TO BUDGE FROM THE CHAIR, EVERYTHING I touched was covered in dust. I was sure that man who claimed to be my uncle considered the dark gloomy office his personal mausoleum. It was a dead space filled with ghosts, crammed with trinkets that must have seemed valuable to him, things he kept to convince himself he'd made something of his life. He probably didn't allow his wife to enter or touch anything, let alone clean, and who knows what one might find in the stacks of paper that were piled everywhere. Before I could sit in the chair, I had to remove and place on the floor some notepads and old papers and a cup of coffee that was acquiring a life of its own.

I'd seen him maybe a couple of times, and during the years my mother lay ill in bed, motionless and losing more and more weight, he hadn't even sent her a bouquet of flowers. The man seemed more dead than alive, yet he insisted on talking nonstop. I thought: when will his excuses end? It was obvious that neither of us enjoyed each other's company. Maybe he was feeling guilty now that Mother, his little sister, had passed away, he'd never spared a cent to help with her medicine. Fortunately she'd always been thrifty and had some money put away in a jam jar she kept behind her headboard. I used it to buy donkey milk from the pharmacy, for her to gargle. To assuage his conscience, as soon as we buried her, he tried to find me a job, somewhere I could make a living, it never occurred to him to take me in. My wife and I, he told me, as if his wife had any say in that household, my wife and I, he said, as if he cared what his wife thought or wanted or believed, probably just using her to apologise, to shirk responsibility, the way men do with the women they know will keep quiet and tolerate lies so as not to disappoint them ... we thought the right place for you, now that my sister, my dear sister, is gone, would be the Hospice of Santa Magdalena. Worst of all, the man truly thought this was the best solution. To force an orphan like me, accustomed to caring for a woman who had lived close to death for two years, to look after other orphans no one expected anything of, except their own deaths of course, for them to free up a bed at the corpse factory. I felt a deep weariness, the only thing I wanted was to leave that room.

I didn't breathe easy again until I found myself alone on that street in Barcelona. And not just because I'd stopped inhaling the fug of tobacco smoke that was everywhere in that house, that seemed to have settled in the shadows, blackened by the melancholy soot of his apathy, though the man hadn't lit a cigarette in my presence, but because I no longer had to put up with anyone or pretend to be grieving. I could suffer my pain any way I pleased. In my hand I gripped the suitcase that a week before had contained bottles of tincture and now held only a few oranges wrapped in my mother's dresses. In my other hand was the folded paper with the address of the hospice, tied to a tiny bag of aniseed that the desperate and silenced woman had prepared for me on her husband's orders. That scrawny Black Madonna of a woman, consigned to oblivion in a house full of votive candles and smoke, her face filled with resentment from mourning the child her husband had not given her ... I didn't even know her name, but I still remember her with compassion. It's strange, I never saw her again, and that afternoon she only appeared a few times, invading our conversation with her loud silence, spying on us from behind the door and enlivening our exchange with a coughing attack both my uncle and I pretended not to hear.

It was cold on the street, the weather was bad, but it hadn't started raining. My hands felt like inert balls of ice. They hurt, and the suitcase was heavy, but I couldn't stretch my fingers and I couldn't switch hands. I had no choice but to endure the weight that was rending my muscles, the backache that made me stoop. I didn't really know where I was headed, and I didn't want to ask for directions. Near Plaça de Sant Jaume, my uncle said. I'd ask when I was there. I liked the bustle on the street at that hour, all the wagons coming and going, their wheels painting the slippery cobblestones that looked as if they needed rain. With all the commotion I went unnoticed, few men pestered me, and the knot in my stomach didn't worsen. I'd never been scared of men, but when they murmured obscenities at me, for some reason I didn't answer back, and when they complimented me I smiled although I was disgusted. When I reached Plaça de

Sant Jaume I didn't know where to go. I dropped the suitcase and one of the corners came apart as it hit the ground. My fingers couldn't fix it, they were stiff and frozen. I tried to wiggle them, but the more I opened my hand to wake them, the more they burned. When the pain lessened a bit, I snapped the string that held the paper with the address, but as I was about to unfold it I noticed a man shouting in a corner of the square. He was going hoarse begging for a few coins to buy bread. I walked over to him and handed him the little packet of aniseed, and he shouted at me, If you got no money, get out. I was scared, and the aniseed scattered on the ground like so many pearls from a broken necklace, and I ran until I bumped into a woman who asked me where I was going in such a hurry. I hadn't recovered from the fright and couldn't speak, so I handed her the note, and she opened it and lowered her gaze and said she couldn't read. I took the paper and read the address to her and she told me where to go.

When I got there, that scoundrel of a custodian was waiting for me with a broom in his hand. A drizzle had started to fall and everything was muddy. He recognised me right away. I suppose it was easy to spot me with my frightened face, and besides I hadn't dawdled so I was on time. To kill time while he waited for me he'd been sweeping, on either side of the stone steps he'd gathered into piles lots of dirty leaves, dog hair, and other bits I couldn't identify. I could see that the broom had been used to sweep several times in any number of directions. The place had a terrible smell. The steps were worn, but the street wasn't as narrow as I anticipated, and the sign over the entrance could still be read quite clearly from the pavement: HOSPICE OF S NTA MAGD ENA. Pigeon droppings covered the remaining letters. Maybe with a bit of luck the street would be wide enough to diffuse all the noise and allow me to sleep. Maybe with a bit of luck I would have a windowless room. You'll see, you'll like it here. I'm told you know how to look after people, the man said. And as he spoke his cheeks lifted, the skin on his face tightened, and he seemed to be holding back a laugh. His presence bothered me. Isn't that so, my girl? I'm sure you'll enjoy it here. I was tired, and to calm the unease the man was causing me, I tried to convince myself that I was imagining things. That after spending so much time alone I needed to get used to sharing my life again. That was all. We're assigning two of them to you, he told me, you'll see, you'll enjoy your time with them. I sensed there was malice in his voice, but I thought perhaps it was me who was soft in the head, maybe my spirit had been sickened by spending all that time with a woman who was terrified of dying and spoke only when her mind wasn't clouded by anguish. You'll see how easy and agreeable they are, and only two of them, my girl, you won't have too much work on your hands. You'll see. But I didn't want anything to do with anyone yet. I wanted to drop into bed and yield to my exhaustion, to the pain in my chest that I'd been hiding for two years and was only getting worse. I see you're not much of a talker, and my goodness, so very young, you should be smiling all day! I didn't know how to get him out of my room. I was beginning to think he was going to suggest that we pray together, but he finally left me alone and told me not to worry, told me to rest. He'd see to it that one of the women came to wake me.

I didn't need anyone for that. I'd been awake for two hours when they knocked on my door, and not because the sky had shuddered with thunder all night, but because I'd dreamed that my mother was alive again; her swollen legs made her scream in pain, and I had to take her hand and administer a few tablespoons of medicine. I didn't know what time it was, but I knew I hadn't slept. I'd closed my eyes for a while but I was exhausted. I'd tossed all night under those prickly blankets, covered my head with the pillow to escape the light from the window, the anguished sorrow that wouldn't let me weep.

The knock on the door came as a sort of salvation. I knew they would put me to work and I would finally stop thinking. In the hallway I encountered a plump woman who looked me up and down as if measuring my height. She told me to go down to breakfast when I was dressed. I didn't want to talk to anyone and no one introduced me either, but everyone had their eyes on me. I had buried my mother only two days before and I didn't have the energy to eat. The smell of warm, over-boiled milk turned my stomach. But I took the glass with both hands, breathed in deeply, and took a few sips so no one would think I was rude. I was so queasy I fell into a daze, the custodian had to call my name two or three times. I asked him where I should leave the coffee and bread I hadn't touched, and he told me not to worry, he was eager for me to meet my charges. Someone else, another woman, would clean up. Not him. I had a bad headache. I wanted to hit myself to see if the pain would stop, but I couldn't with everyone watching.

I followed him down the hallway, and before we reached the room, again it seemed to me that the man was repressing a smirk. For a moment I thought I was going mad, I had to stop thinking poorly of everyone. When we got to the room where my charges were waiting, everything smelled of urine. The floor was covered with newspapers that were yellowed and stuck to the tiles. A long-haired old man sat naked on the floor in the corner where he'd pissed. On a bed was another man of uncertain age who also seemed a wreck, for when I walked through the door and greeted him he didn't appear to see me. The first was Angelet, the second Tomàs. I asked the custodian if they had already had their breakfast. There's not enough for everyone around here. Not everyone can eat, my child. In order for some to eat, others must go hungry. Such is life, you'll see. You think they realise? He didn't bother to repress his snigger. I wanted him out of there.

At the hospice we followed the same routine every day. I liked it because it kept me busy and I only felt my grief at night, and besides I'd learnt a few tricks to help me cope. One was to go without food for a couple of days. The pain in my stomach was so bad it overpowered everything else, it masked the grief of losing my mother. I didn't eat the bread and boiled potatoes the cook gave me; when no one was looking I slipped them in my pockets and gave them to that pair of dullards. If the juices stained my smock as I made my way to their room, that night I soaked it in water and rubbed it clean. I draped it over a string that I hung across my room, and in the morning it hardly smelled. I had grown accustomed to Angelet's urine, so the odour wasn't that strong. I'd had two years to become used to it; my mother wet her bed sometimes and woke with an embarrassed look on her face, and as we had no money to send the sheets out to be cleaned,

I just turned the mattress. I undressed her, washed and hung the nightdress on the balcony, then laid her on the dry part of the sheet. That's why sometimes I'd walk into our little flat and the entire place seemed to be coated in urine. It's dense, difficult to get rid of, that smell.

I hadn't been in there a month before they had passed sentence on me. In their eyes, the trial period to determine whether I was trustworthy was over, and now I belonged to the group that did not merit being addressed. The custodian taunted me openly. I heard you were served up some good hot chocolate today, eh? They all laughed brazenly. Over time, I'd come to realise that evil is like morphine. At first a little is enough, but then you need more and more to feel good, especially if you have an audience you don't want to disappoint with your insults and vulgarity. Did you have a taste? Of the chocolate, I mean. Or did it make you lose your appetite? What they didn't realise was that I preferred to clean up Angelet's shit—it coated the entire room after one of his episodes, it was everywhere except the bedpan, surprisingly he never touched that—than having to sit with them in one of the big rooms and listen to their banal prattle. They thought they were punishing me, locking me in there with those two men no one wanted to touch, but they did me a favour. It meant I didn't have to endure the kind of conversations I'd suffered my whole life. I was tired of pretending. At first even my mother's illness was like a balm, it gave me an excuse to sequester myself in the house and not deal with anyone. An excuse no one questioned. I won't deny that sometimes I was scared I would end up a bit touched in the head, friendless, with something inside me that would make me the saddest person. But time helped me to accept myself and stop suffering. Only occasionally was I overcome by fear, but after a few days it would lift, it was a matter of survival.

Nihil novum sub sole, the Bible says. The pigs in the hospice were just like the rest, only they were locked up in there, and I was too, so I couldn't avoid them. The only thing that calmed me was going into that room and listening to those two men, cleaning them up, or turning the key to my own room and waiting for sleep. The pigs continued to have their fun, day in, day out, they thought humiliating me and refusing to speak to me was punishment, they didn't know it saved me, it allowed me to be on my own and not have to strive to make sense of their boring nonsense. At least Tomàs and Angelet no longer wanted to be someone, and they didn't want to prove themselves to anyone. They were free because they didn't care about their pride or what others thought of them. They had accepted that no one would ever see them again, they could let their madness run free. Their fantasies were more interesting than the dull empty words of those who believed they were fascinating and only ever talked about what others allowed them to. As if they, too, weren't touched in the head. At the hospice, the ones who thought themselves free were actually enslaved, only that pair of accursed men had been able to escape banality. The poor souls in the big rooms had not avoided their own moral decline, some of them also mocked and taunted others. They looked down on Angelet and Tomàs because they could still soap their own bodies and didn't meet the morning drenched in urine. To me they were nothing more than vulgar dimwits, people who had spent too long in the world of the living and hadn't accepted their new condition, so they needed to bolster themselves at the expense of others. But they had entered the world of the damned now, just as Tomàs and Angelet had, and I too. The sooner they realised, the sooner they might discover the rewards of their new condition.

Every morning, Angelet told me that a sparrow had alighted on his hand and serenaded him. Always the same sparrow. As soon as he heard my footsteps approaching, he sat at the head of Tomàs's bed and stuck his hand through a hole in the window where someone had hurled a stone before I arrived at the hospice. Angelet would scold me tenderly, my entrance had frightened away the sparrow, he said, a few seconds before it had been sitting in his hand. I would remove his arm from the hole in the glass and tell him to stop putting it there, one day he'd cut himself. I collected the newspapers I had spread on the floor the previous night, for him to pee on, wadded them up and plugged the hole in the window, to see if Angelet would change his story once and for all. But the next day the man had tossed the paper ball into the street and stuck his hand through the window. More than a game, it had become a habit, and after two weeks of this I was starting to tire of it. But he was having fun, and I loved him and wanted to make him happy. That's why I kept up my performance every morning when I opened the door, and he'd let out a hearty laugh that quickly turned into a cough.

Tomàs, on the other hand, had more imagination. At first he even frightened me a bit. When he had those bouts of insanity he pulled out his hair and was left with bald spots for weeks. I soon realised that the strange things he said concerned a woman he had loved, he needed to vent and didn't wish me any harm. I knew it was him, he kept on saying. My father and Pere would have beaten me up, as men do. Maria and the boy would have kept quiet. He's the only one who would have hurled that tomato at me. Sometimes I didn't understand a thing, he would start talking about turnips and end up talking about pears. But I liked listening to him as I cleaned his bedsores, it occupied my mind and distracted me from the darkness inside me, and it taught me, a city girl, a lot about country life. Jon never understood us. He thought it was something it wasn't, and so he left, but it wasn't what he thought it was. He didn't understand us, because people can't understand what they don't try to understand. We loved each other. She wanted it as much as I did. That's why I had to put an end to his suffering, you understand? He was my brother and I was his, and my duty was to end his suffering. Blood obligations they were. He couldn't continue to suffer like that, and he would never have understood because not even I could explain it. I didn't know how to, you see? I had to put an end to that pain.

Every day Tomàs revealed more; bit by bit I assembled the pieces, as if fitting together torn scraps salvaged from the rubbish heap, and slowly they grew into a love story. Sometimes I feared the tale would end and I wouldn't know how to fill my time. I was grateful when his thoughts got stuck on a fragment of the story that he'd repeat all week. I still had nightmares, the loss of my mother still tormented me. I wasn't ready to leave the hospice. Where would I go? I knew I was too young to have such sadness, but I didn't know if I'd ever be rid of it. I was comfortable with the two men. I could weep or be silent and not feel judged. She was the one who started it, he told me. I must have been about twelve or thirteen years old. Jon and Pere had already been born. Yes, they'd been born. They weren't young children anymore. I remember it well. The two of them had gone hunting for wild mushrooms with Father and I'd stayed home to look after her because she was ill. Take good care of her, my father told me. But I was bored. A farmhouse so empty, a boy so young, so many chores and no one to force you to do them ... you see what I mean. It was early and I was bored. I went up to see how she was. And yes, she was sick, shrivelled up like a raisin on the edge of the bed, wrapped in an old blanket as if she wanted to hide. What's wrong? I asked. She didn't respond. I stretched out next to her. The mattress was cold. She lay there, bundled up and still. A heaviness came over me, and when I woke up she was staring at me. She was still covered with that thing, but not completely, her forehead and messy hair were showing, her eyes peered at me. You're the only man I could allow to lie with me like this. You know that, don't you, Tomàs? I was happy to hear I was her favourite. You're a good boy and you'll be a good man. She took her arm from the blanket and slipped it inside my trousers. And she said, You like it, don't you? I did like it. Then I would say to Tomàs, Shush now, enough! Those things are between you and your beloved. Don't be so crude! And he: see how she was the one who started it? She wanted it too. Jon got it all backwards. That morning I kept getting harder. Larger. And she kept telling me, You're the only man I let lie with me like this. You like hearing that, don't you? When Tomàs started with his obscenities I ran away pretending to be angry. I didn't want to know what he'd done with that woman, but I noticed I was wet down there and it embarrassed me. I had to go freshen up again because I felt dirty. Country folk have always been a bit much. And he: she didn't have to tell me that it should be our secret. I knew what we were doing was frowned upon. But we weren't afraid. In some ways part of my body was hers by birth, you know? Whenever we could find a moment we were at it. Ay, for God's sake, stop this talk! But it wasn't all a bed of roses. One day, that half-formed thing with one arm and a stump on the other side came along, and I was jealous, because it looked like me. Because he was my son. But he sucked on her tits. On those tits that were mine. And I knew she knew that I hurt him in the crib, she could see the bruises, no one could pretend they weren't there, but she never scolded me, and I never went near her any more. I wanted to punish her for spending her time with that stunted little thing that only cried. I wanted her to devote herself to me again, and be mine. We didn't touch each other for a few years. And when the boy started walking, I told her I didn't want him near my fields. If she wanted me to touch her again she had to let him run wild like an animal, because that's what he was. She could give the others any explanation she wanted, but that thing wasn't to set foot in my fields. I came first. I decided. You understand? Then she was mine again. Only mine. And the boy? What happened to the boy? Didn't you get married? She passed away. One day she fell over, I wasn't prepared for that moment, and she was dead. And if I couldn't touch her, no one should be able to touch her.

Because she was mine, mine alone. She told me so herself. I promise, she always told me so. And the best way to protect her was burning her. I had to turn her into smoke. Then no one else could touch her. But Jon wouldn't have understood that either. I'm sure he wouldn't have understood.

TABLE OF CONTENTS

NÚRIA BENDICHO (BARCELONA - CATALUNYA, 1995)

I don't remember the first time I felt I had to write. I must have been eight or nine years old. It wasn't a mere impulse, but an obligation. I felt I had to be a writer, no matter what it took. My grandfather, who died the year before I was born, left me a large collection of classics of Catalan literature. I dusted them off and devoured them, working my way through writers such as Víctor Català, Aurora Bertrana, Miquel Llor, Juli Vallmitjana. I began to value my own tradition, and felt my heartbeat quicken with every page. Then I turned to Spanish realism, later French naturalism. I stumbled—by chance or luck—on Faulkner, and discovered his disciples. I had found my natural interests: poverty, illness, exploitation, the condition of women, the question of evil. The authors I admired shared similarities that I, too, wished to capture and make mine. I needed to pay homage to those from whom I had learnt not only the art of writing, but also, and most importantly, to observe the world around me deliberately, philosophically, with a critical eye. Literature is nothing more than the craft of applying fresh brushstrokes along the path the masters have laid out for you.

MARTHA TENNENT AND MARUXA RELAÑO ARE A MOTHER-daughter translation team. They have translated a number of works from Spanish and Catalan, including *War, So Much War* and *Garden by the Sea*, by Mercè Rodoreda, *Blood Crime*, by Sebastià Alzamora, and *The Sea*, by Blai Bonet. They are both recipients of National Endowment for the Arts fellowships for their translation work. Martha was previously dean of the School of Translation at the University of Vic, Barcelona. Maruxa worked as a journalist in New York and was a translation editor for the *Wall Street Journal*. They live in Barcelona.

We translate female authors who write in minority languages. Only women. Only minority languages. This is our choice.

We know that we only win if we all win, that's why we are proud to be fair trade publishers. And we are committed to supporting organisations in the UK that help women to live freely and with dignity.

We are 3TimesRebel.